DECORATIVE
FRAMES

Miranda Innes

DECORATIVE FRAMES

Photography by Clive Streeter

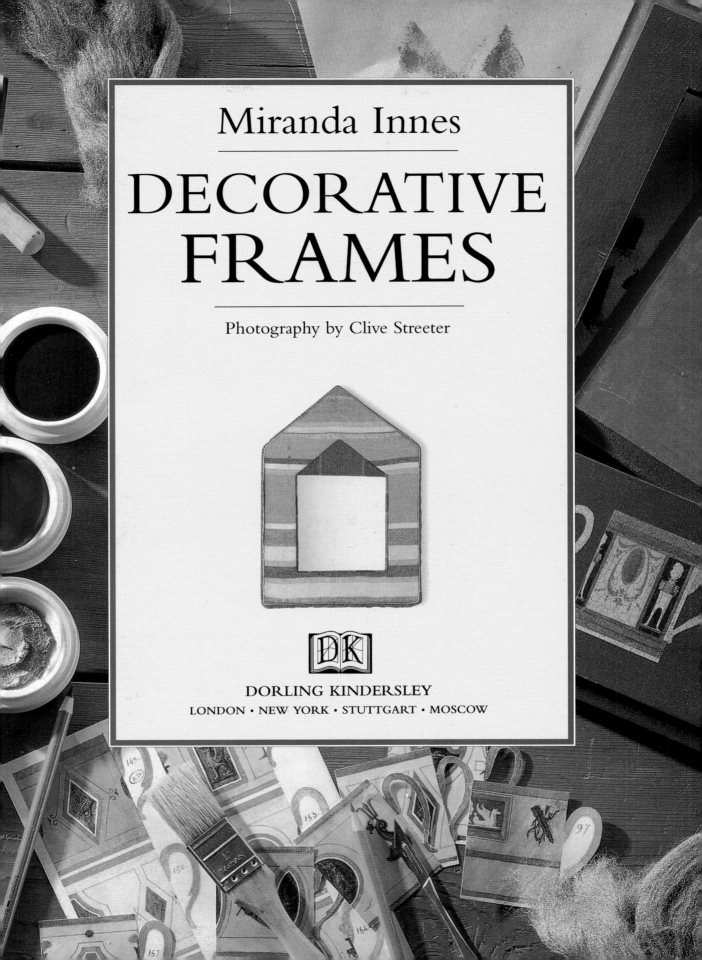

DORLING KINDERSLEY

LONDON · NEW YORK · STUTTGART · MOSCOW

A DORLING KINDERSLEY BOOK

Created and produced by
COLLINS & BROWN LIMITED

First American Edition, 1995
2 4 6 8 10 9 7 5 3 1

Published in the United States by
Dorling Kindersley Publishing, Inc.
95 Madison Avenue
New York, New York 10016

ISBN 0-7894-0336-6

A catalog record is available from the Library of Congress.

Project Editor	Heather Dewhurst
Managing Editor	Sarah Hoggett
Editorial Assistant	Corinne Asghar
U.S. Editor	Laaren Brown
Art Director	Roger Bristow
Art Editor	Marnie Searchwell
DTP Designer	Claire Graham
Design Assistant	David Drew
Photography	Clive Streeter
Stylist	Ali Edney

Reproduced by CH Colourscan, Malaysia
Printed and bound in France by Pollina

Contents

Introduction 6
Basic Techniques and Finishes 8

Wood and Metal Frames

Introduction 11
Antiquated Paper 12
Driftwood and Seashells 16
Stars and Hearts 20
Glazed Wood 24
Jeweled Silver Frame 28
Touches of Gold 32
Glittering Trail 36
Rustic Chicken Frame 40
Baronial Candle Sconce 44
Ideas to Inspire 48

Paper and Fabric Frames

Introduction 53
Fishes and Squiggles 54
Folk Stitches 58
Golden Birds Mirror 62
Tiny Hooked Frame 66
Brilliant Tissue Frame 70
Pure Fabrication 74
Gothic Mirror 78
Gilded Velvet Frame 82
Ideas to Inspire 86

Templates 90
Contributors 94
Index 95
Acknowledgments 96

Introduction

FRAMES are a decorator's dream: they make your works of art feel at home; they elevate undistinguished prints into something noteworthy; they can make a motley collection of fond memorabilia take on a more dignified form; and, if they are surrounding a mirror, they make a flattering foil for your face.

Frames work well in a room, much like jewelery or accessories; strong, matching, or harmonizing frames can highlight motifs from the existing decor or echo a color scheme, bringing all the elements together like a musical fugue. If you do not possess quite enough courage to call yourself an artist or painter as such, you can always sidle toward being one by surrounding it with a frame that emphasizes all of its shapes, colors, and images, creating a whole emphatically greater than the sum of its parts. Without too much effort — and with no

Foil Finesse
Humble components assembled with dash for a jewel of a frame.

Waterworks
A watercolor seascape perfectly moored amid driftwood.

great pretensions — you will have created something that is well worth looking at.

Frames are surprisingly easy to make. I am not talking of store-bought frames — often so neat, predictable, and bland that you do not actually see them at all. This book is full of frames that you can make yourself and embellish upon, frames with character, charm, and frames of which you can be justifiably proud. If your finished frame engulfs the print you made it for, so what? Put the print at the back of the closet, install a mirror in the frame in its place, and bask in glorious reflections.

In order to make a frame, you need little in the way of raw materials: a few lengths of cheap lumber or even just cardboard, and some paint, paper, fabric, and glue. You will be able to find most of the more interesting ingredients around your home, lying unused in drawers or scrapbags. You might be galvanized into action by a significant birthday, a new baby, or your parents' wedding anniversary. All the cards and the

Kindest Cuts
Copy, cut, and color — the photocopier is your friend

beautiful wrapping paper, the ribbons and bows too full of memories to throw away might persuade you to arrange them tentatively on a sheet of delicate handmade paper. If your collage is successful, you might then feel encouraged to do it credit with a frame rich with decoupage, cut from the wrapping paper, or with a papier-mâché frame made from the bright tissue that packaged the champagne glasses.

Rhythm in Blue
Elegant Italianate lettering adorns a papier mâché frame.

Beautifully framed memories are so much more meaningful than an assortment of photos and cards stuffed away in a drawer or box in the attic.

All kinds of things benefit from being dressed up this way. You can remind yourself of a blissful time in the country with a collage of photos, fall leaves, the check from dinner, and the label on the wine bottle, set in a simple wooden frame of russet and gold. The souvenirs from a trip to the seaside – shells, pebbles, postcards, and saltwater taffy – will look terrific when they are surrounded by sea-washed driftwood. Once you have embarked on the frame-making trail, plain unadorned wood

Scrap Happy
Curvaceous shape in card covered in rich cloth.

will begin to look naked and unfinished. Your fingers will itch to transform all the unadventurous rectangles around your home with spots of gilding, stencils, or subtle and seductive wood stains.

Ready-made frames are very cheap, and save time and trouble as a basis for your creative flurries. Let someone else go to the trouble of cutting perfect miters that do not fall apart. You have much interesting things to do – such as trying your hand at mosaic. You probably thought that huge expertise was required, but with just a simple idea and plenty of patience you can experiment with glorious glittering tesserae bought from a store, or recycle the shattered remnants of your beautiful blue and white Spode dinner service. Or you might undertake an adventure in kitsch, using fragments of a mirror and glass gems bought from a bead shop.

All sorts of things go into constructing frames, and frames can be made from all sorts of things. With this book and a dash of ingenuity, splendid surroundings are yours for the asking.

Regal Rags
Hand-hooked from scraps – a recycler's crowning glory.

Basic Techniques and Finishes

To MAKE a good picture frame you need the right tools and equipment. The essential tools are: craft knife, metal ruler, backsaw and miter box, clamps, hanging fittings, and nylon cord. You will also need these materials: wooden molding, mat board, polyvinyl white glue, gummed packing tape, hardboard for backing, and glass cut to size.

Measuring and making a frame

First decide on the size of your frame. Measure the length and width of the picture or mat, if any, then add ⅛ in (3mm) to each measurement to allow for fitting. Add the two measurements together and multiply this figure by 2 to give you the total length. To allow for molding which projects beyond the picture at the corners, multiply the width of the molding by 8 and add this to the total. Finally, add on 2in (5cm) to allow for cutting. This figure is the total length of molding you should buy. It is best to buy molding in one length rather than two, in case there are slight discrepancies in the manufacture.

Accurate measuring is vital when cutting the frame. Always measure along the outside edge of the molding to find the point to cut. The length of each side, therefore, should be the length or width of the picture plus ⅛ in (3mm), plus twice the molding width.

Each piece should have mitered corners running in opposite directions. Check as you work that you are cutting the pieces correctly. After mitering the corners, do not sand them, even though the edges might feel rough, because they will not fit together properly. Leave sanding until after the frame has been assembled. For extra reinforcement, you can hammer two panel nails into each corner.

Decide how much of your picture you want to show, then add 2-3in (5-7.5cm) for the mat borders. Cut out the mat for the picture using a craft knife or mat cutters. Cutting a beveled edge may take practice; using mat cutters makes the job easier – the blade is set at the correct angle and is adjustable to accommodate different thicknesses of mat board.

Finishing the frame

To hang the picture, screw hanging hooks in each side of the frame, about a third of the way down from the top. Then tie nylon cord across the back, making sure it is neither completely taut, nor so slack that the cord will be seen above the top of the frame.

Once you have made your picture frame, you can leave it as it is with the wood-grain visible, or use one or more paints to produce an interesting finish, a range of which are illustrated below.

◀ Fine, even lines are produced by pulling a long-haired brush through wet glaze.

◀ This frame was stained around a stencil and the resulting pattern was outlined in black paint.

◀ A verdigris effect is achieved by sponging mint-green paint over a dark gray base, then sponging gold paint sparingly on top.

◀ This repetitive stenciled pattern was painted in gold on a black ground. The paintwork was rubbed back to age it.

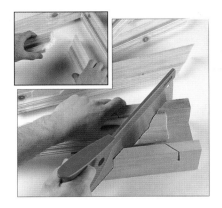

1 *Holding the molding in the miter box, saw one edge to a miter running in the right direction. Measure the length of the frame. Cut the second mitered corner so that it runs in the opposite direction. Cut three more lengths. Glue the mitered ends together (see inset).*

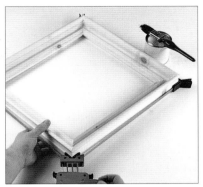

2 *Place the frame in a clamp to hold the sides together. The best type has three L-shaped corner brackets and a fourth adjustable bracket, and nylon tape running around all the sides. Place the corner brackets on, tighten the tape, and leave the frame in the clamp overnight.*

3 *Draw the dimensions of the mat on the reverse of a piece of mat board. Holding a metal ruler along the outer line as a guide, cut along the line with a craft knife in one fluid movement. Cut out the mat window, holding the knife at an angle of about 60° for a beveled edge.*

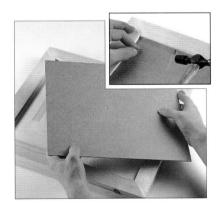

4 *Tape the picture to the reverse of the mat. Assemble the frame by inserting the glass cut to size, then the mat and picture, facedown, and hardboard cut to size for the backing. Hammer small nails into the sides of the frame to secure (see inset).*

5 *Stick gummed packing tape around the edges of the hardboard and frame to keep out dust and moisture. Using a bradawl to make holes in the wood, screw two hanging hooks into the sides of the frame. Tie nylon cord across the back and knot it firmly.*

6 *The frame is now complete. Check that the hanging cord is not visible from the front, and hang the picture on the wall.*

◄ *Pull a comb through wet glaze for a striped pattern.*

◄ *Several paint glazes are applied onto a surface and softened to produce faux tortoiseshell.*

◄ *Stenciling is one of the most effective paint techniques.*

► *This variation of the combing technique produces an interesting wavy pattern.*

► *Ragging over a strongly colored wet glaze creates lively patterns.*

Wood and Metal Frames

WOOD IS THE TRADITIONAL material for frames. As a starting point, visit your local building supply store with an eye to exploiting all those fascinating varieties of beading and molding to make your frame. Lacquer, verdigris, dragging, stippling, and craquelature are effective traditional finishes for wood, but there are other ideas you can try: a kaleidoscope of variations on a mosaic theme; a collage of sparkling foil and jewels; stencils inspired by African tribal art; or a scrapbook of decoupage. Or you can be really bold, and try your hand at making a metal frame. Start small and economical, and as your confidence increases so can the size of your frames.

Antiquated Paper

MATERIALS

Wooden frame
Red acrylic latex paint
Candle
Green acrylic latex paint
Decorative paper motifs
Polyvinyl white glue
Water-based craquelure (two solutions)
Raw umber artist's oil color

EQUIPMENT

Sandpaper
Artist's brush
Steel wool (without soap)
Craft knife
Cutting mat
Small manicure scissors
Paper towels
Cloth

NOTHING BEATS DECOUPAGE for quick and easy effectiveness, and it provides an instant way to jazz up a plain wooden frame. We are surrounded by images begging to be snipped from magazines, gift wrap, greeting cards, and catalogs, and recycled as part of our own personal memorabilia. Tickets, invitations, fond messages scribbled on the corner of a newspaper – these can all do service in this pack-rat art.

With decoupage you can be clever, witty, nostalgic, or pretty – the choice is yours. Try to make sure that there are common denominators of color to help marry image and background. Likewise, having a textured background will prevent your decoupage motif from standing out too glaringly.

Careful cutting is all-important in decoupage – tiny curved manicure scissors can handle tricky curves, while a craft knife will make easy work of the rest. Remember that craft knives are razors and are lethally sharp, and use a cutting mat or piece of cardboard to protect your work surface.

Ruff and Scumble
Marie Vignon, this splendidly bedecked figure, presides with a coy smile over a Tudor snack. The dark and distressed red and green of the frame is close in tone to the portrait, and the graphic refinement of the Napoleonic coffee cups parallels that of the finely detailed ruff and bodice.

Decoupage Decoration
Photocopied engravings can be aged in tea or painted with watercolor. The chunky vegetables taken from ancient seedpacks would make an appropriate frame for an award from your local flower or farm show. Decoupage is a great opportunity to coordinate picture with frame.

Decorating the Frame

The joy of decoupage is that it is very easy to do, you know what it will look like, and with very little effort you can produce something convincingly sophisticated.

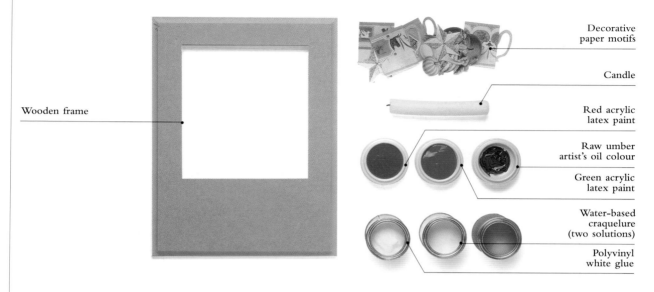

Decorative paper motifs

Candle

Red acrylic latex paint

Raw umber artist's oil colour

Green acrylic latex paint

Water-based craquelure (two solutions)

Polyvinyl white glue

Wooden frame

1 *Rub sandpaper wrapped around a block over the surface of the wooden frame to smooth any rough edges and give the surface of the wood a slight key. Mix red acrylic latex paint with water until it is the consistency of cream and apply a coat over the front of the frame. Allow to dry.*

2 *Rub a candle over the entire surface of the frame to coat it with a layer of wax. Then wipe off the excess flakes of wax.*

3 *Mix green acrylic latex paint with water to the consistency of cream and apply a coat over the front of the frame. Allow to dry. Rub a pad of steel wool in a circular motion over the entire frame (see inset). This will remove some of the green paint and expose the red paint underneath.*

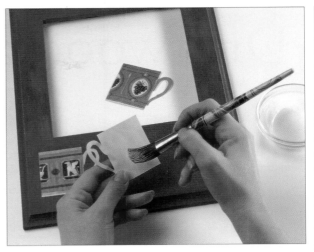

4 *Select your motifs to decorate the frame. These can be color-copied to the required size or used as they are. Paint a layer of diluted polyvinyl glue over the motifs and allow to dry before cutting them out. This strengthens the paper and helps prevent tearing. Cut out the motifs using a craft knife and cutting mat for straight edges, and a pair of small manicure scissors for curves.*

5 *Arrange the paper motifs on the frame until you are satisfied with the design. Brush the back of the motifs with diluted polyvinyl glue and glue them in positon on the frame. Dab a scrunched-up paper towel over the motifs to smooth out air bubbles and absorb any excess glue. Make sure that all the edges are stuck down. Leave to dry.*

6 *To create the antique look of cracked varnish, apply one coat of water-based craquelure over the frame and allow to dry. (Craquelure is usually sold in two solutions, and it is advisable to follow the manufacturer's instructions.) Apply a second coat (for fine cracks) and allow to dry. Finally, apply a coat of the second solution. Allow to dry. Colorless cracks will slowly form across the surface.*

7 *Using a soft cloth, rub a large blob of raw umber artist's oil color into the cracks over the surface of the frame. Rub off the excess paint with the cloth and buff the frame to polish it. The dark color will stay in the cracks to create an aged look.*

Driftwood and Seashells

MATERIALS
Driftwood

Rope

Length of wood, ¾ x 1½in (2 x 4cm) thick

Polyvinyl white glue

Nails (optional)

Glass

Mat

Hardboard, for backing

4 frame turns and screws

2 screws, ½in (12mm) long

Seashells

Seaweed

EQUIPMENT
Ruler

Saw

Clamp

Screwdriver

Craft knife

Cigarette lighter

BEACHCOMBING IS ONE of life's great pleasures, and nothing is such an effective antidote to trouble and stress as walking along the seashore, collecting shells and flotsam, and listening to the sound of the waves. The charm of these driftwood frames lies in their rugged and weather-beaten nautical texture, an appealingly countrified character, and muted color, which flatters all sorts of pictures from a moody sepia photograph to the most delicate watercolor painting.

Driftwood frames are the perfect choice for rural retreats and are a welcome recollection of wide open spaces for city dwellers. With their subtle understated appearance, they fit in easily with natural colors and fabrics, as well as hold their own in more sophisticated interiors.

For the designer, the charm of driftwood frames lies in their spontaneity – no two pieces are ever the same. The design has to be guided by the materials, a process requiring the same careful concentration as putting together a jigsaw puzzle. It is this feature that makes every driftwood frame unique.

Flattering Flotsam
The wider your choice of driftwood the better – smooth, rounded pieces, perhaps with remnants of paint, give a subtle finish; small, jagged, twiggy pieces are more rustic. The two can be combined, and any amount of seashells, pebbles, or dried seaweed can adorn the frame. To complete the seaside theme, flaunt a little flotilla on the shelf beneath.

Shorelines
Winter, with a biting wind and immediately after a violent storm, is the most fruitful time to search along the sandy coast for treasures from the sea. This frame then becomes a souvenir along with the delicately evocative watercolor.

Making and Decorating the Frame

A pleasure to put together from a seaside treasure trove, this driftwood frame would be the perfect souvenir of a summer idyll.

Wood, ¾ x 1½in (2 x 4cm) thick

Driftwood

Seashells and seaweed

Nails

Polyvinyl white glue

Rope

Mount

Hardboard backing

Glass

Screws and frame turns

1 *Collect pieces of driftwood and rope from a beach. Select pieces of a manageable size. Leave the driftwood in a warm place, such as a sunny windowsill, to dry. This may take a few days if the wood is damp.*

2 *Saw the wood into four pieces, two measuring 8in (20cm) long, and two measuring 10in (25cm) long. Using polyvinyl glue, stick the pieces of wood together to make a frame. Let it dry in a clamp (see p.9) for at least four hours. The corners can be nailed for extra security, if preferred.*

3 *Using polyvinyl glue, glue pieces of driftwood onto the frame, covering the front, outer sides, top, and bottom of the frame. Choose interesting-looking pieces of driftwood and let them overlap the edges of the frame. Don't worry if there are gaps between the pieces — these can be filled later with shells or seaweed.*

4 *Lay the frame facedown and, working from the back of the frame, glue several thinner pieces of driftwood to the inner sides of the frame, covering only half the width of the wood. These thin strips will form the rabbet of the frame to hold the picture and backing in place. Leave the frame to dry for approximately 24 hours.*

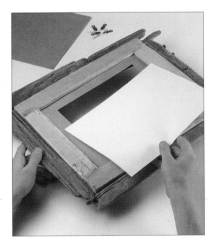

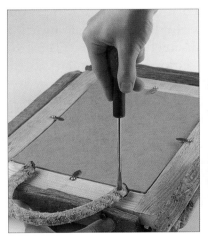

5 *Lay the frame facedown and carefully insert the glass, mat, and picture, all cut to size, in the back of the frame. Check from the front of the frame that the picture is centered within the frame and mat. Place the hardboard backing on top of the picture and secure in place by screwing in one frame turn in the center of each side of the frame.*

6 *Using a craft knife, trim the rope to a length of approximately 8in (20cm). This will form the hanging hook for the frame. Singe the ends of the rope with a cigarette lighter to keep it from unraveling. Then screw the ends of the rope to the back of the frame, positioning them above the hardboard backing and an equal distance from each side edge.*

7 *Turn the frame the right way up and fill in any gaps in the driftwood decoration by gluing in seashells and pieces of seaweed. Allow the frame to dry.*

Stars and Hearts

MATERIALS

Paper
Wooden frame
Acetate
Black, green, and red
acrylic latex paint
Gold powder
Polyvinyl white glue
Water-based acrylic
varnish

EQUIPMENT

Pencil
Ruler
Waterproof
felt-tip pen
Craft knife
Paintbrush
Sponge
Hole punch
Small dish
Varnish brush

S TENCILS ARE ALL THINGS to all people; in the days of flower power, when the word "natural" meant all was right with the world, stenciled roses erupted on walls, trailing honeysuckle wreathed wastepaper cans, bunches of grapes burst from filing cabinets, and morning glory twined about bathrooms. One tended to feel akin to a browsing aphid among the greenery.

Stencils have since moved on, and, with a grateful nod to their traditions in 18th-century Britain and North America, they are flourishing as a convenient and easy method of repeating a design. Aesthetically, stencils capture a contemporary approach to decor, being both casual and precise. They lend themselves to subtle blends of color and soft uneven paint techniques. Strong tonal contrasts have a naive charm, while stippled muted designs work well with faded tapestry. It is child's play to steal motifs from favorite fabrics in a discreet visual pun. Ethnic textiles can be echoed in color and pattern to their mutual enrichment. The secret is to use broken color — flat color on a plain background looks too harsh.

Patchwork Granny
The strong plain colors and geometric shapes of Amish patchwork quilts transfer well to stencils and make a fitting border to a revered ancestor who might well have turned her hand to quilting.
The Amish were particularly fond of using black — usually somewhat faded — as a foil to bright color. Here the background is more of a dark earthy gray; pure black would be too extreme.

Three Easy Pieces
The only tricky aspect with stencils is getting a repeat pattern to "behave" at the corners. If your frame is square, this simplifies matters. Otherwise it is best to work from the corners and use a single central motif to fill gaps.

Decorating the Frame

Cutting tiny shapes is tricky; if you want a small motif as punctuation, you can raid your office for a hole punch to make miniature circles. Failing this, small squares or triangles are manageable with a craft knife.

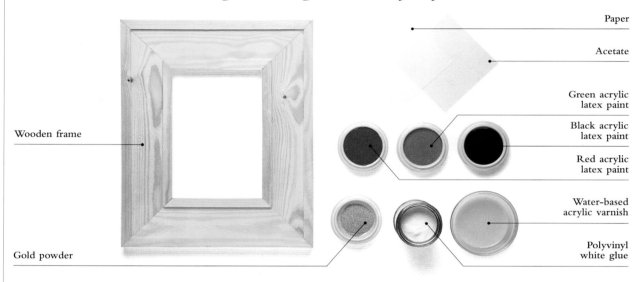

Paper

Acetate

Green acrylic latex paint

Black acrylic latex paint

Red acrylic latex paint

Water-based acrylic varnish

Polyvinyl white glue

Wooden frame

Gold powder

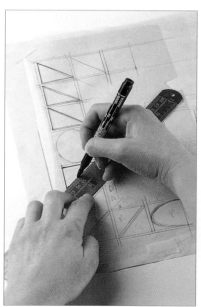

1 *Using books or magazines as reference, sketch out a design for your frame. This symmetrical design comprises triangles and ovals, the sizes of which were worked out to fit the dimensions of the frame.*

2 *Draw the design onto acetate using a waterproof felt-tip pen. Make sure that you leave enough "bridges" or strips of acetate between each shape. Cut out the shapes carefully with a craft knife.*

3 *Paint the frame, including inner and outer edges, with a coat of black acrylic latex. Let dry.*

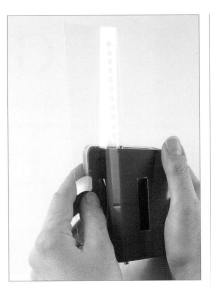

4 *Position the acetate stencil on the frame and tape it in place. Dip a sponge in green acrylic latex, dab off the excess, then sponge over alternating triangles and the side ovals of the stencil. Don't worry if you dab some paint onto other areas of the frame — this can be touched up later.*

5 *Cut out another stencil for the alternating red triangles. Position the acetate over the frame, lining it up accurately. Sponge red acrylic latex over the remaining triangles and ovals. When dry, touch up the frame with black acrylic latex as necessary. Let dry.*

6 *Next make a stencil of a row of dots. A simple and effective way to do this is to use a hole punch, which saves laborious cutting with a craft knife*

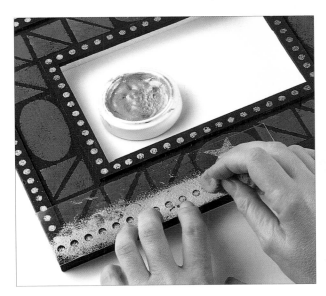

7 *Mix some gold powder with polyvinyl glue in a small dish. Position the dot stencil on the inner edge of the frame and sponge gold lightly over the stencil. Repeat on the outer edge of the frame. Allow to dry.*

8 *Make star and heart stencils for the ovals of the frame. Position on the frame, then sponge gold over each stencil in turn. When the frame is dry, apply a coat of varnish.*

Glazed Wood

MATERIALS

Length of wood, 2 x 1in (5 x 2.5cm) thick

Polyvinyl white glue

Wood filler (optional)

Beeswax furniture polish or petroleum jelly

Acrylic paints

Mirror, 17½in (44cm) square

Cardboard,17½in (44cm) square

4 mirror corners

Brown packing tape

2 mirror plates

Screws

EQUIPMENT

Ruler

Saw

Housepainter's brush

Coarse-grade sandpaper

Screwdriver

THE VICTORIANS had a curious and misplaced passion for woodgraining – it is hard to see why one should labor to simulate perfect grain patterns when one can so easily enjoy the natural look of wood as it comes, with all its knots and irregularities. The natural grain on this wooden frame has been accentuated using layered transparent tones of blue-green paint, while the knots in the wood have been picked out with beeswax as a resist. It would be a challenge to find anything simpler than these four pieces of wood, but the result has a quiet sophistication that requires nothing more.

Try using different dilutions of water-based paint in shades of one color or in wildly contrasting colors, or use color over a base of wood stain, dye, or even ink for more variation. With a technique of such simplicity, using such easily available materials, you can feel free to try out whatever idea comes to mind.

The casual exploitation of the intrinsic texture and qualities of wood is accentuated here by the use of antiqued silver-leaf mirror glass. You can buy this in various finishes, or the brave can experiment and make it themselves.

Romantic Reflections

The irregular silver-leafed mirror in this frame gives a gloriously soft-focus reflection and has an intriguing texture that makes plain mirror glass look unutterably dull in comparison. Lilies and a blackened silver candelabra emphasize the elegance of this simple frame.

Muted Pewter Colors
Softer and quieter colors are wonderfully effective in summoning up a look of times long past. It may seem obvious, but there is nothing to stop you from hanging your mirror vertically or horizontally as best fits the space you have.

Making and Decorating the Frame

This wooden frame, which is as simple as can be, exploits the natural pattern and texture of humble pine planks.

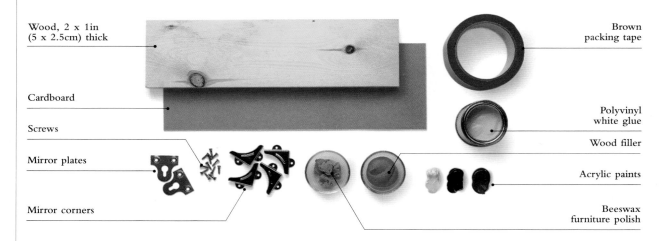

Wood, 2 x 1in (5 x 2.5cm) thick

Cardboard

Screws

Mirror plates

Mirror corners

Brown packing tape

Polyvinyl white glue

Wood filler

Acrylic paints

Beeswax furniture polish

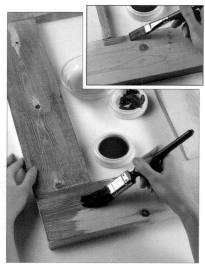

1 *Saw the length of wood into four pieces, two measuring 17in (42.5cm) long, and two measuring 14in (35cm) long. Assemble the frame by gluing the four pieces of wood together using polyvinyl glue. Let dry overnight with weights on top.*

2 *Fill the corner joins of the frame with wood filler if necessary. Rub the frame down thoroughly with coarse-grade sandpaper to remove any rough edges and unevenness in the wood. Using your finger, apply small blobs of beeswax furniture polish or petroleum jelly on any knots in the wood and rub in with your finger to spread the wax on the surface. Let the frame dry overnight.*

3 *Apply a coat of blue-green acrylic paint diluted 1:3 with water over the front of the frame. Where the wax has been applied, the paint will be resisted. Allow the paint to dry, then turn the frame over and paint a ½in (12mm) blue-green border around the inner edge of the frame (see inset). This is to prevent the pale color of the wood from being reflected when the mirror is inserted into the frame.*

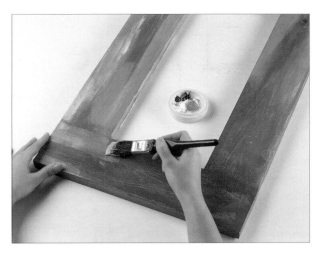

4 *When the first coat of paint is dry, roughly brush on a coat of lighter blue-green paint, together with some streaks of white, and let dry again.*

5 *Rub sandpaper over the entire frame to expose some of the layers of paint and create a distressed effect. Rub the sandpaper more vigorously over the knottier parts of the wood so that these become more apparent.*

6 *To soften the distressed effect, cover the whole frame with a wash of the original blue-green acrylic paint, this time diluted 1:4 with water.*

7 *When the paint is completely dry, turn the frame over and position the mirror over the central hole. Place the cardboard on top of the mirror and secure in place with a mirror corner screwed to each corner. Tape the edges of the cardboard down with brown packing tape. Finally, screw one mirror plate to each side, 7½in (19cm) from the top of the frame.*

Jeweled Silver Frame

MATERIALS

Thick cardboard
Double-sided adhesive tape
Picture
Acetate
Foil
Flat-backed glass jewels
Glass beads
String
Superglue

EQUIPMENT

Pencil
Metal ruler
Craft knife
Ballpoint pen
Scissors
Bradawl

MAKING THIS jokey, flamboyant frame — with a supervising adult to wield craft knife, Superglue, and bradawl — is just the thing to keep fractious children quietly occupied on a rainy afternoon. The materials are cheap and easy to come by, and the technique lends itself as much to wiggly infant scribbles as to fastidious Celtic curlicues drawn by an expert hand.

This particular frame is tiny, just large enough to accommodate a shocking pink valentine. The big frosted beads and glowing spheres of molten glass give this little frame a dash of color and refine the silver and glass in amusing contrast to the hank of coarse twine from which it hangs. You could use the same method to make a more generous-sized frame, or you could change the shape to a heart, diamond, circle, or whatever you prefer. If you make the "window" any shape other than square or rectangular, you will have to use an extra strip of foil to cover the cardboard, which will show through.

Completely Foiled
There is nothing pretentious about this little picture frame. Quickly and easily put together, it is cheerfully reminiscent of the punched and embossed tinware from Central America. It works well with bright colors and ethnic textiles.

Hearts on Show
These two slightly more dignified frames were made using heavier aluminum foil, which is harder to come by and use but has greater resilience. The pendant heart was made by wrapping foil around a cardboard shape.

Making and Decorating the Frame
Quick, easy, and fun to make, this frame is the perfect sparkly setting for favorite memorabilia.

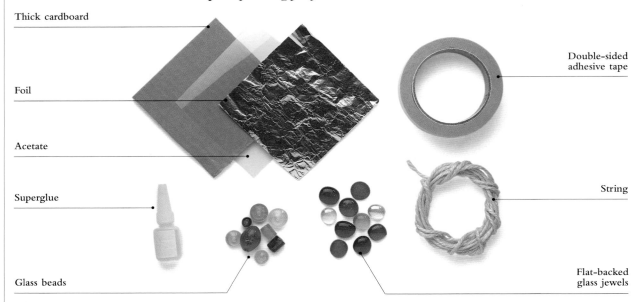

Thick cardboard

Foil

Acetate

Superglue

Glass beads

Double-sided adhesive tape

String

Flat-backed glass jewels

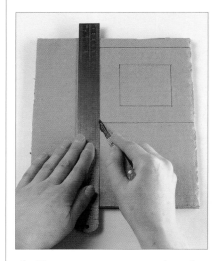

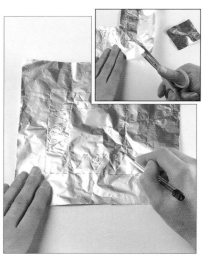

1 *Draw two squares on a piece of cardboard and cut them out using a metal ruler and craft knife. Cut out and discard a smaller square from the center of one to form the opening of the frame. This cardboard square will be the top square of the frame*

2 *Using double-sided adhesive tape, stick a picture in the middle of the bottom cardboard square. Then stick a piece of acetate, ½in (12mm) smaller all around than the cardboard square, over the top of the picture.*

3 *Using the scissors, cut out a square of foil 2in (5cm) larger on each side than the cardboard squares. Using a ballpoint pen, draw shapes on the foil within the frame area to create a raised pattern on the reverse side. Cut out the central opening ⅛in (3mm) smaller on each side than the opening in the top square of cardboard. Make a diagonal cut in each corner (see inset).*

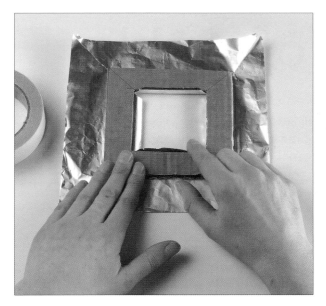

4 *Using double-sided adhesive tape, attach the top piece of cardboard to the foil, positioning the openings so that they match exactly. Fold the inner edges of the foil into the opening in the top piece of cardboard.*

5 *Attach the bottom piece of cardboard, with the picture facing downward, over the top piece using double-sided adhesive tape. Stick pieces of tape around the edges of the foil, and then fold these outer edges back over the cardboard frame to secure, tucking in the corners neatly.*

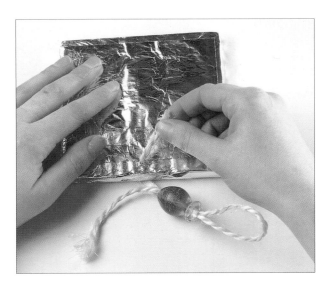

6 *Turn the frame the right way up and, using a bradawl, carefully pierce a hole through the top of the frame, from front to back. Make a hanging loop by threading two glass beads onto a loop of string. Thread one end of the string through the pierced hole in the frame from front to back. Knot the ends together and seal with Superglue.*

7 *To complete the frame decoration, glue brightly colored glass jewels to each corner on the front of the frame with Superglue. Let dry.*

Touches of Gold

MATERIALS

Wooden molding
Polyvinyl white glue
Wood filler
Black wood stain
Mat board
Oil-based gold paint
White acrylic paint
Cardboard
Backing cardboard
Nails
Brown packing tape
2 hanging hooks
Decorative cord

EQUIPMENT

Miter box
Backsaw and clamp
Sandpaper
Housepainter's brush
Craft knife
Pencil
Artist's brush
Stippling brush
Steel wool
Cloth

THIS ELEGANTLY UNDERSTATED FRAME is the perfect starting point for frame making, and the method can be used to produce something as grand or as folksy as you want. If you have ever been mesmerized by all the different kinds of beading and decorative molding sold in building supply stores, and longed for some way of exploiting this treasure trove, your problem is solved. A container of glue and a few short lengths for experimentation, and you can produce multiple variations using different moldings and wood stains. Accuracy in cutting and mitering the lumber is important. If you can use the specific equipment for frame making, you will not need recourse to quantities of wood filler and your finished frame will have a look of professional smoothness.

Experiment with combinations of different wood dyes and acrylic overcoats to achieve subtle veils of color that will coordinate with your decor and any photographic print you want to use. Here the delicate striations and moiré effect of the wood showing through the color give a surface richness that is satisfying without being overwhelming.

Candlelit Classic
The warm flickering light of candles is just the thing to bring the medallions and flakes of gold to life on this simple frame and to play up the lively pattern of the wood.

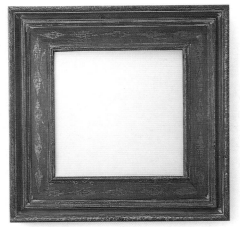

Variations on a Theme of Wood
The same all-purpose frame-making technique can be employed with subtle variations of color and differing proportions to make a satisfying group.

Making and Decorating the Frame

Simple to make and darkly effective, the mysterious glitter and stipple of this frame would adapt well to different moldings and colors.

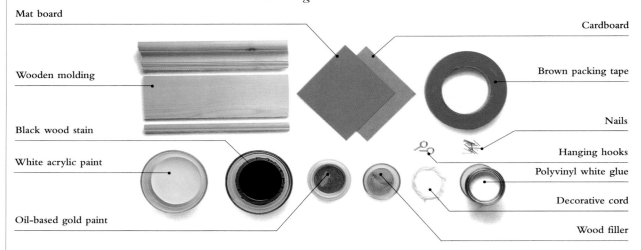

Mat board

Wooden molding

Black wood stain

White acrylic paint

Oil-based gold paint

Cardboard

Brown packing tape

Nails

Hanging hooks

Polyvinyl white glue

Decorative cord

Wood filler

1 *Make a basic frame from wooden molding (see pp. 8–9). Build up this basic frame by gluing on a wider outer frame and a narrower inner frame, using different moldings, to create a three-layered frame. Leave in a clamp to dry overnight (see p. 9).*

2 *Fill in any holes in the joints with wood filler, then rub the frame with sandpaper to smooth down rough edges. Paint a layer of black wood stain over the frame using bold sweeping strokes to cover the area quickly.*

3 *Make a simple stencil by cutting out a circle from a piece of mat board using a craft knife. The circle should be small enough to fit the width of the frame. Use the stencil to draw a circle at intervals around the frame, pressing hard with your pencil to make grooves in the wood.*

4 *Using an artist's brush, carefully fill in the penciled circles with gold paint. The paint will collect in the penciled grooves, adding to the decorative effect of the stenciled pattern.*

5 *Dip a stippling brush or sponge in the gold paint, dab the excess paint off on a piece of cardboard, then dab the brush randomly over the frame for a decorative broken pattern. Let the frame dry.*

6 *To soften the black and gold coloring, apply a coat of white acrylic paint over the front of the frame and leave to dry.*

7 *Rub the paint back using steel wool. Then buff the frame with a soft cloth to bring up the gold. Insert the mat, picture, and backing cardboard in the back of the frame, securing with nails and brown packing tape (see p. 9). Attach hanging hooks and cord to finish (see p. 9).*

Glittering Trail

MATERIALS

Particleboard, ¼ in (6mm) thick, for base

Particleboard, ⅝ in (16mm) thick, for sides

Polyvinyl white glue

Mirror

Water

Silver smalti

Vitreous glass tesserae

Tile grout

Mirror plates and screws

EQUIPMENT

Ruler

Backsaw

Housepainter's brush

Clamps

Felt-tip pen

Craft knife

Safety goggles

Tile nippers

Rubber gloves

Squeegee

Cloth

Bowl

Screwdriver

MOSAIC IS A MYSTERY until you realize that the little pieces of mirror or ceramic tile – the tesserae – are glued first, and then the filler is smoothed over the top. This is a naughty modern invention, far quicker and more manageable than the traditional direct method (where the tesserae are individually embedded in mortar) or indirect method (where the tesserae are stuck facedown to strong paper and then bedded in mortar in panels).

Having grasped this basic principle of mosaic, you may wish to plunder the Roman repertoire of geometric borders and strong, vigorous designs for replication on your frames. The Romans had a thoroughly impressionist way with color, and a cheerful opportunism when it came to materials. Faceted glass jewels, amethyst quartz, and mother-of-pearl discs sit quite happily with colored and gold glass squares (smalti to you and me). For a more contemporary source of inspiration, you could take a trip to Barcelona to study the astounding work of Antonio Gaudí. Here, at last, is a use for those heart-breaking accidents with the dishwashing.

Snail's Pace

For those who do not spring energetically to life in the morning, the contemplation of a meandering snail, leaving a glittering silver trail, may bring comfort to those early ablutions. A mutable spectrum of different greens makes a congenial background; the more variations of a single color you can lay your hands on, the livelier the finished effect will be.

Gastropod at Large
With the dogged persistence typical of snails, this specimen has escaped its boundaries and is making for the open spaces. This snail has been hand-painted on a tile, using the raku technique.

Making and Decorating the Frame

*Using this unorthodox method, assembling the piece into a
design is quick and easy. As you gain confidence, you
might wish to experiment with pebbles, shells, glass gems,
or prized pieces of broken china.*

Polyvinyl white glue

Vitreous glass tesserae

Particleboard for sides

Mirror

Silver smalti

Particleboard for base

Vitreous glass tesserae

Tile grout

Mirror plates and screws

1 *Construct a simple frame from
particleboard. Carefully cut out a
rectangular base using a backsaw; saw
four side pieces to fit. Using polyvinyl
glue, glue two side pieces on the base
to make a right-angled corner. Glue
the mirror onto the base, butting it
right up to the corner, then glue on
the remaining two sides. Clamp the
frame and let it dry overnight.*

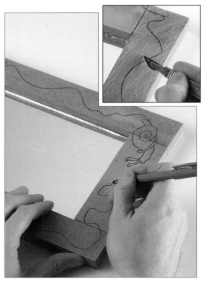

2 *Seal the frame with a mix of 1
part glue to 1 part water; allow to
dry. Draw a design on the frame with
a felt-tip pen. Here the artist has
designed a snail with its trail going
around the frame. Choose a design
that has good color contrast. Score the
frame with a craft knife (see inset) to
roughen the surface. This helps the
mosaic adhere.*

3 *Using tile nippers, cut the
silver smalti into small pieces.
These will be used for the snail trail.
Always wear safety goggles when
using tile nippers, as pieces of smalti
can fly everywhere.*

4 *Apply a bead of polyvinyl glue along the marked trail of the snail. Lay pieces of smalti along the glue, butting up the pieces to one another. Use the mosaic nippers to "nibble" the smalti, cutting it up into smaller shapes as desired.*

5 *Make the snail using a mixture of yellow, orange, and brown tesserae. To build up the pattern, start at the center of the snail shell and spiral outward. Finish with the snail's head and antennae.*

6 *Apply polyvinyl glue along the inner rim of the frame, then stick down green-colored tesserae so that they jut up slightly over the edge. This will allow the tesserae that is to be applied on top of the frame to butt up against them, making a neat edge.*

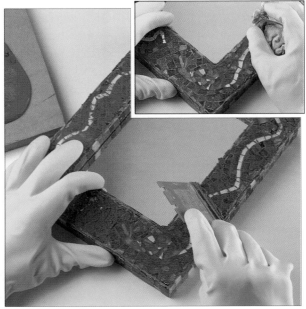

7 *Apply tesserae to the outer edge of the frame in the same way. Then build up the green patterning on the top of the frame, following the curve of the snail trail to create movement and flow. Use the tile nippers to shape the tesserae as you require.*

8 *Let the completed mosaic dry for a day. Mix tile grout to mud-pie consistency, or use ready-made grout. Wearing rubber gloves and using a flexible squeegee, apply grout generously over the frame. Clean the grout off the frame using a cloth dipped in cold water and wrung out (see inset). The grout will remain in the areas between the tesserae – the interstices. Let dry, then attach mirror plates on the back (see p.9).*

Rustic Chicken Frame

MATERIALS
Tracing paper
Driftwood, 1in (25mm) thick
Plywood, ⅜ in (9mm) thick
Wood glue
Tacks
Oil paints
Turpentine
Copper
Nails
Thin wire
Mirror
Cardboard
2 mirror plates and screws

EQUIPMENT
Pencil
Coping saw
Hammer
Housepainter's brush
Artist's brush
Tin shears
Piercing saw
Pliers
Screwdriver

THERE IS NO REASON why frames need to be serious. This pair of hens has a wayward sense of humor that will appeal to all but the most earnest. The frame is carefully constructed so that the frisky chicken candlesticks can slide from side to side, though, somewhat perversely, they are positioned so that it is impossible to reflect their candlelight in the glass. However, you could lengthen the slots in the base of the frame if you passionately wished to use the sconce in the traditional way – to maximize candlepower.

Despite its insouciant air, this is a fairly difficult frame to make, and accuracy is essential in the cutting and assembly of wood and copper. However, the reward is a witty mirror frame with a weatherworn, countrified look that will always make you feel like whistling something from *Oklahoma!* If these ornery old speckled hens do not appeal to you, you might research the charms of the dapper Scots Dumpy, the elegant Silver Spangles, or the rich russet of the familiar Rhode Island Red. A visit to a farm museum will reveal that there is a lot more to chickens than simply beaks and wattles.

A Tale of Two Chickens
Beak to beak, wattles rampant, these two bucolic birds double as doughty candle-bearers on this witty mirror frame.

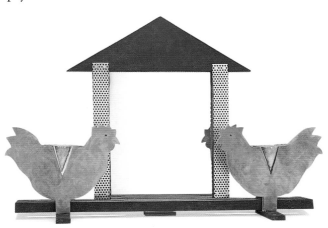

Metallic Mirror
For a more high-tech variation, the clucking confrontation takes place in front of a nifty neo-Palladian mirror embellished with punctured metal pilasters.

Making and Decorating the Frame

Textured driftwood and plywood chickens are used in this whimsical mirror sconce, which, despite its carefree air, is one of the more complicated frames to tackle. Make sure that the wood is cut accurately so that all the elements of the frame can slot together smoothly.

Copper

Cardboard

Plywood, ⅜in (9mm) thick

Tacks

Mirror plates and screws

Nails

Thin wire

Oil paints

Wood glue

Driftwood, 1in (25mm) thick

Turpentine

1 *Photocopy the templates for the frame (see p.90) to the required size. Trace templates A to C onto driftwood and templates D to G onto plywood, and cut them out with a coping saw. You should have 12 components.*

2 *Using wood glue, glue the two uprights (C) into the slots in the base of the frame (B). Glue the roof (A) to the top of the uprights, making sure they are level.*

3 Make the runners for the chickens. Glue and then tack piece G to piece F to make an L shape. Glue and then tack the chicken to piece F so that it is 1½in (3cm) away from piece G. Repeat to make the second runner.

4 Insert the runner into the base of the frame so that piece G protrudes through the slot. Glue and tack piece E to the top of piece G and the side of the chicken to fasten the runner in place. Repeat to attach the second runner to the base.

5 Paint the frame base, uprights and roof, both front and back, with blue oil paint diluted to the ratio of 1:20 with turpentine, and let dry. Paint the chickens with diluted orange oil paint and again let dry before painting more.

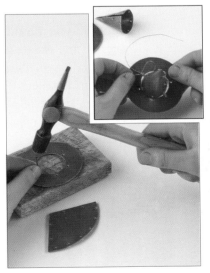

6 Using an artist's brush, stipple a mix of orange, cadmium red, yellow ochre, lemon yellow, and white oil paint over both chickens. Paint details such as eyes and beaks on the chickens' heads.

7 For each candlestick, photocopy the templates H and I (see p.90) to the required size and trace onto copper. Using tin shears and a piercing saw, cut out each shape. Make holes as marked with a nail and hammer. Bend piece H to make a cone and place it on piece I. Loop thin wire through the holes to fasten (see inset).

8 Turn the candlesticks the right way up and nail them in place on the chickens. Insert the mirror in the back of the frame, add the cardboard backing cut slightly larger than the mirror, and fasten in place with nails (see p.9). Attach mirror plates to the back of the mirror to finish (see p.9).

Baronial Candle Sconce

MATERIALS

Thin steel
Candle
Mirror
Beeswax furniture
polish
Blackening cream

EQUIPMENT

Tracing paper
Pencil
Tin shears
File
Fine-grade wet and
dry sandpaper
Block of wood
Hammer
Tin punch
Soldering iron
Straight-edged pliers
Round-nosed pliers
Cloth
Steel wool

NOT EVERYONE has a soldering iron lurking in the bottom of a cupboard. On the other hand, if you do happen to acquire one, you will be able to effect miracle cures for flea-market finds, such as broken tin trunks and antique hatboxes with torn hinges, as well as making the odd baronial frame or two.

Metal frightens people quite unnecessarily – once you get the hang of it, and learn how to use it safely, you will find it no more problematic than cardboard and a good deal more malleable and handsome. Nothing beats glinting dark metal for drama, and it is a wonderful material to explore. You can cut it, mold it, shape it, give it texture, puncture it, and it will remain obediently as you want. Then you can blacken it, polish it, or simply leave it plain.

If you are nervous about committing yourself to sheets of steel and equipment, you could begin your experiment with just a pair of tin shears and a couple of cans. Try embellishing a plain wooden frame with a few pieces of tin laid flat and nailed to the frame. Carefully done, this is a thrifty piece of recycling that looks surprisingly good.

Deceiving Looks
This frame would look just right in the echoing hallway of your Gothic mansion, were it not for its diminutive size – it is only 7½in (18cm) by 4¾in (11cm). Tiny and perfectly formed, it is the ideal excuse to try your hand at simple metalwork.

Sun, Moon, and Dolphins
This eager dolphin will forever be bouncing through the waves under a composite celestial emblem. And for those who believe that mirrors should be hidden, you can put doors and spikes on a little mirror, as a reminder of the perils of vanity.

Making and Decorating the Frame

This hammered and textured dark metal frame, with a flickering candle flame reflected in its mirror glass, could bring a sense of drama as well as a touch of the castle to your humble abode.

Thin steel

Beeswax furniture polish

Blackening cream

Candle

1 *Photocopy the templates for the frame (see p. 91) to the required size, and trace them onto a piece of thin steel. Cut out all the components using tin shears. File all the edges straight, then rub with fine-grade wet and dry sandpaper.*

2 *Place a corner piece (C) onto a block of wood, and punch a pattern of studs into it by hammering a tin punch into the metal at regular intervals. Repeat with the three remaining corner pieces.*

3 *Solder the four side pieces (A and B) together at the corners to form the basic frame. Solder the corner pieces onto the frame with the studs protruding upward (see inset).*

4 *Solder the five spikes (E) onto the semicircle (D), ensuring that they are spaced evenly. This will form the base of the candlestick at the front of the mirror frame.*

5 *Using straight-edged pliers, bend the small strip for the candlestick (F) at a right angle. Then bend it around a candle using round-nosed pliers. This forms the top part of the candlestick. Make sure there is at least a ⅛in (3mm) "stem" to hold the candle away from the mirror. With the round-nosed pliers, curl the spikes of the candlestick base downward. Solder the candlestick pieces onto the center base of the frame (see inset).*

6 *Using straight-edged pliers, carefully bend the four mirror backing corners (G) into shape. These will hold the mirror in place on the back of the frame.*

7 *Place the mirror facedown on the back of the frame, making sure there is a ½in (12mm) overlap all the way around, and solder the mirror plates in position to secure the corners. Then bend piece H into the shape of a hanging hook and solder it in place at the top center of the back of the frame.*

8 *Rub a soft cloth dipped in a little beeswax furniture polish over the sides of the finished mirror frame, but not the corners, to bring out the shine. Buff with a soft cloth.*

9 *Still using a soft cloth, rub blackening cream onto the frame corners. Then buff the corners with steel wool and wet and dry paper to highlight the decorative effect of the pattern of raised studs.*

Ideas to Inspire

Wood and metal frames provide a starting point for a wealth of decorative effects in frame making. As the frames in this section demonstrate, you can make a frame from any type of wood and leave it untreated, decorate it with paints or mosaic, or cover it with shells, trinkets, tin cans, copper foil, string, cinnamon sticks, metal studs, or anything else you desire. Above all, experiment and have fun!

▼ **Tiny Box Frame**
This simply constructed box frame, measuring 5in (12.5cm) square, is decorated with a combination of pencils, crayons, pens and paints, to make a perfect match with the ceramic figure set inside.

▲ **Wood on Wood**
Made from driftwood, this frame relies on textural contrast for impact, juxtaposing sea-battered driftwood with a smooth, sanded wooden base. The carved wooden avocet is attached to the frame by delicate metal legs.

▶ **Paint and Pigment**
Constructed simply from pieces of old wood, this frame is painted to echo the colors of the Mexican doll collage, then rubbed with gold pigment and sealed with varnish.

◀ **Lettered Frame**
A simple wooden box frame is transformed with a coat of acrylic gesso and a wash of acrylic paint, then decorated with lettering and drawing pencil.

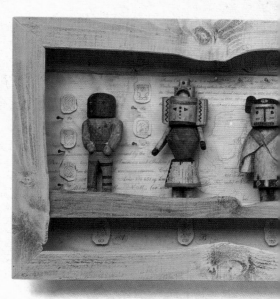

◄ Kitsch Delight

Starting with a chipboard base, this mirror frame is first covered with crumpled gold foil, then decorated with a jumble of shells, buttons, sequins, and pieces of glass. Gold furnishing studs surround the heart-shaped mirror.

► Colorful Arch

This arched mirror frame is decorated with pieces of broken china, in a range of greens, blues, and purples, held together with blue-colored grout.

► Clean and Simple

This tactile box frame is constructed entirely from driftwood and has received no treatment other than a thorough sanding by hand to achieve its ultra-smooth finish, in perfect partnership with the minimalist painting within. Its clean, simple lines convey a great sense of balance.

▼ Adrift at Sea

A single piece of driftwood, with characteristic peeling paint and rough-textured edges, has been cut to make this simple yet effective frame, used to display a nautical needlepoint picture.

▶ Wired Sunburst

A dainty sunburst of six wire rays is soldered to a wire circle. Added decoration comes in the form of a glass blob suspended by finer wire in the center of each ray.

▶ Slate Mosaic

This chunky mosaic frame is made from an assortment of smalti, vitreous glass, broken plates and tiles, and slabs of slate. They are attached to a wooden frame using tile adhesive for the ceramic pieces and silicone adhesive for the slate.

◄ Fishy Frame
First stained with watercolor paint, this wooden frame was then decorated with glue stars and swirls, pieces of foil, candy wrappers, cellophane, and sequins, before being further embellished with acrylics and gold paint.

► Valentine Mirror
This folksy frame, made from hand-painted particle-board, decorated with colorful fabric hearts and circles, would make the perfect Valentine's Day gift.

▼ Beaten Metal Frame
This unusual homage to scrap metal was made by nailing beaten sections of tin cans around a wooden frame. The tin was then burned with a blowtorch to achieve an aged patina.

▲ Stenciled Drama
Simple to do, this frame achieves great dramatic impact with its use of different paint textures and strange birdlike stenciled motifs set against its dark background.

Paper and Fabric Frames

·······································

YOU DO NOT NEED a hammer and nails to make a handsome frame; cardboard, fabric, paper, and glue can do just as well, and give free rein to your creativity. This section is devoted to the decorative potential of paper and fabric in frame making. Papier-mâché is cheap and adaptable, and it is a great starting point for fancy paintwork or three-dimensional designs. A patchwork of sumptuous fabric remnants can be shown off to advantage as a frame. This is your chance to surround your image with a painter's repertoire of color and a couturier's dream of silk, satin, velvet, and braid. Good taste or radiant excess is yours for the stitching and gluing.

Fishes and Squiggles

MATERIALS

Plywood, ½in (12mm) thick
Plywood, ¼in (6mm) thick
Polyvinyl white glue
Tacks
Paper
Water
Matte oil-based paint
Silver metal leaf
Decorator's acrylic gloss varnish
Mirror
Cardboard
Nails
Brown packing tape
2 D-ring hangers

EQUIPMENT

Pencil
Ruler
Coping saw
Sandpaper
Hammer
Scissors
Large bowl
Blender
Spatula (optional)
Housepainter's brush
Varnish brush
Screwdriver

PAPIER–MACHE is a wonderfully simple way to give character to plain plywood and to add three-dimensional motifs to a flat surface. Paper pulp, which can be molded to any shape, has been used on this frame to create fish and squiggles for a frisky seaside flavor. You could make a mirror with hearts and arrows for the love of your life, or astrological signs combined with sun, stars, and moons for anyone with a taste for the occult. Whatever design you choose, remember to keep it simple – the effect of the hand-molded shapes highlighted with silver metal transfer is bold and dramatic, and attempting something much more complex will lessen the impact, as well as drive you to extremes of vexation.

This is an exuberant sculptural frame, and not the best one to tackle if you don't like to get your hands sticky. There is no alternative to mixing the paper pulp and glue by hand, and the smoothing and shaping of the surface is best achieved with slightly dampened fingers. On the other hand, squelching paper pulp between the fingers can bring back fond memories of childhood, and making the pulp is as soothing as kneading dough.

Perfect for Pisceans

This cool and uncluttered mirror frame is perfectly at home in a cool and uncluttered bathroom – an obvious but important piece of advice is to seal it thoroughly against steam or accidental dousing in water. This frame would make a perfect gift for any Pisceans among your acquaintances.

Mayan Motifs

These simple shapes, probably based on some prehistoric archaeological find, have a pleasant irregularity and suggest the hand of the maker. In an age of standardized mass production, such touches of personality are something to be prized.

Making and Decorating the Frame

*Vibrant turquoise and silver hieroglyphs
and fish combine to make a frame with an air of
Mexican panache.*

Thick plywood

Thin plywood

Cardboard

Brown
packing tape

Decorator's
acrylic gloss
varnish

Polyvinyl
white glue

Matte oil-
based paint

Silver metal
leaf

Tacks and nails

D-ring hanger

Shredded paper

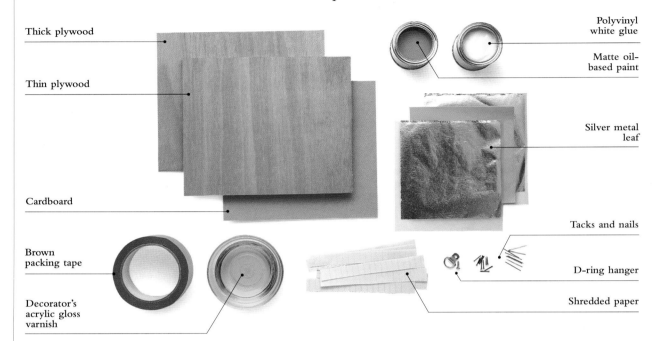

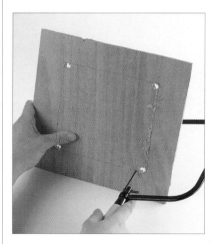

1 Using a pencil and ruler, draw a square on thick plywood. Cut it out using a coping saw. Cut out a square in the center. Sand the edges. Cut out a square of thinner plywood 2in (5cm) larger than the square aperture in the first piece. Cut out a square in this piece ¾in (2cm) smaller than the first opening.

2 Using polyvinyl glue, glue the smaller plywood square over the center of the larger one – there should be a ½in (1cm) overlap around the inner edges of the frame. This is the rabbet to hold the mirror. For extra security, tack the smaller plywood square to the larger one using at least three tacks on each side. Allow to dry.

3 To make the pulp, cut paper into strips and soak it overnight in water. Boil the soaked paper and water for 20 minutes, then liquify in a blender and squeeze until dry. Add polyvinyl glue in the proportion of 2 cups of glue to 1 large bowl of pulp. Mix in well with your fingers to make the pulp smooth (see inset).

4 *Lay the frame with the double side facing up, and spread a thin layer of polyvinyl glue over the surface. Next cover the whole surface with paper pulp, smoothing it down with your hands or a spatula. Allow to dry for 48 hours until the papier-mâché is firm to the touch.*

5 *To decorate the pulp base, first spread a thin layer of polyvinyl glue over the area to be decorated, then add shapes made from wet pulp – here fish and squiggles – molding and smoothing them in position with your fingers. Let the frame dry for 48 hours until solid.*

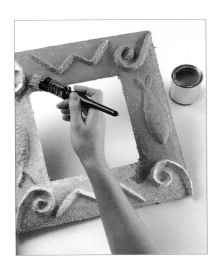

6 *Paint the entire frame, front and back, with a coat of turquoise paint. Allow the paint to dry for at least two hours.*

7 *Apply the silver metal leaf to the relief patterns. To do this, spread polyvinyl glue over the relief areas, then cut the silver metal leaf to size and carefully press it over the relief areas, gently smoothing down with your finger. When dry, coat the silver decoration with a layer of acrylic gloss varnish.*

8 *When the varnish has dried, insert a mirror cut to size in the back of the frame. Place the cardboard backing on top and nail in place (see p.9) to secure. Stick brown packing tape over the cardboard edges to secure more and keep out dust and moisture. Finally, screw in a D-ring hanger on each side of the back of the frame.*

Folk Stitches

MATERIALS

Tapestry yarn:
2 skeins cream,
1 skein red,
4 skeins blue
12-mesh interlock
canvas, 11½ x 13in
(29 x 33cm)
Thick cardboard
Masking tape
Thin cardboard

EQUIPMENT

Tapestry needle
Scissors
Cloth
Steam iron
Pencil
Craft knife
Metal ruler
Pegs

NEEDLEPOINT IS the fashionable pastime for the glitterati of stage, screen, and magazine; its quiet rhythm calms and soothes stressed nerves while waiting for the next moment of glory.

The neat geometric designs suggested by the grid structure of interlock canvas adapt surprisingly well to frames. If you are so inclined, you could probably be very ingenious with computer-aided design and create something personal using your initials combined with a Japanese kimono motif. Failing that, you could raid your childrens' schoolbooks for a few sheets of graph paper and pass many happy hours trying out patterns with colored crayons until you achieve a design you like. Old patchwork is a good source of ideas; stripes, checks, shadowed diamonds, or cubes will all sit well around a frame.

For colors, you are overwhelmed for choice. In any needlecraft store you will find walls composed of hanks of tapestry yarn in the most fastidious gradations of shade and tone. If color excites you, choosing from this heady spectrum is a serious thrill.

Peasant Memories
A piece of pure nostalgia, the likes of this stylish French lady are highly unlikely to be seen today browsing in the Rue de Rivoli. The simple design of this needlepoint frame, reminiscent of the cross-stitch beloved by country people all over the world, has a decided affinity with her complicated embroidered garb.

Tricolor Encore
The same three colors look totally different when their emphasis is changed. The same design with red predominating is much sharper, and the complex design on the square frame has a more delicate impact.

Making the Frame

*Most people stitch in a definite direction, and usually end
up with more of a rhomboid than a rectangle. The answer
is to pull your needlepoint into shape and steam-iron it.*

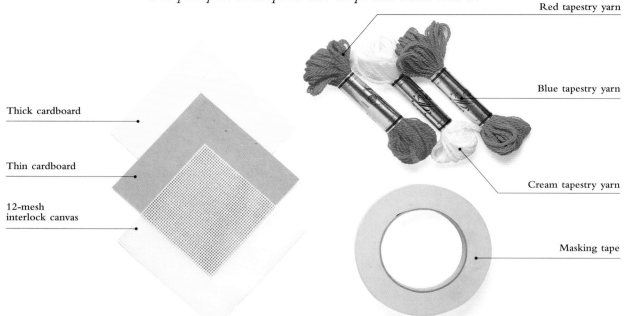

Red tapestry yarn

Blue tapestry yarn

Cream tapestry yarn

Thick cardboard

Thin cardboard

12-mesh
interlock canvas

Masking tape

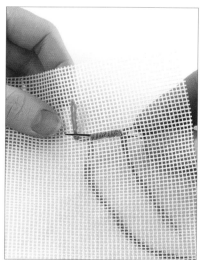

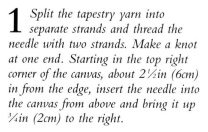

1 *Split the tapestry yarn into
separate strands and thread the
needle with two strands. Make a knot
at one end. Starting in the top right
corner of the canvas, about 2½in (6cm)
in from the edge, insert the needle into
the canvas from above and bring it up
¾in (2cm) to the right.*

2 *Work tent stitch by inserting
the needle in the lower diagonal
square to the left of where the needle
came up. Bring the needle up in the
square directly above. Repeat, working
from right to left. When you reach
the knot, cut it off as you will have
fastened the yarn with your stitches.*

3 *When you reach the end of the
first row, work the next row from
left to right, and so on. The needle
will point alternately upward and
downward with each new row.
Follow the chart on p.91 when
stitching. Each square on the chart
represents one stitch on the canvas.*

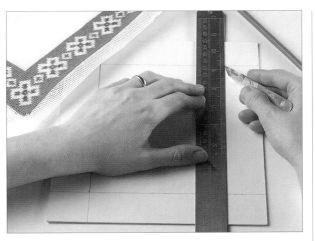

4 To change yarn color, take the needle to the back of the canvas, weave it through a few stitches, then cut off the end. Start with a different color then before and begin with a knot ¾in (2cm) to the left of where you want to begin stitching. Follow the chart to complete the stitching.

5 Trim the edges of the canvas. Press and shape your finished needlepoint with a cloth and steam iron. Draw the dimensions of the needlepoint on thick cardboard, making the finished size two stitch rows smaller all around the edge, to allow the needlepoint to overlap the cardboard when assembling the frame. Using a craft knife and metal ruler, cut out the cardboard frame.

6 Cut out the frame opening in the canvas using sharp scissors. Start at the center and cut out to each corner so that you have four triangular flaps.

7 Place the needlepoint facedown and lay the cardboard frame on top. Fold the triangular canvas flaps over the cardboard and secure with pegs. Check that the inner edges of the frame look neat from the front. You may need to pull the canvas tighter and readjust the pegs.

8 Trim the excess canvas and attach the flaps to the cardboard with masking tape. Trim the outer corners of the canvas, fold over the outer flaps (see inset), and attach with tape. Place a picture facedown, cover with thin cardboard, and tape along three sides.

Golden Birds Mirror

MATERIALS

Paper
Flour and water paste
Gesso
Mirror
Acrylic paints
Thin cardboard
Gold tempera powder
Polyvinyl white glue
Epoxy putty
Mirror plate
Superglue

EQUIPMENT

Scissors
Housepainter's brush
Pencil
Pair of compasses
Ruler
Artist's brush

THIS LARGE circular mirror frame, made of many layers of papier-mâché, is strong and light and exhibits all the interesting irregularities that paper assumes when it gets wet, together with a delicately tattered edge achieved by the layers of paper circles.

Gone are the days when paint had to be matte and flat to be respectable. Here, the broken texture of the paint adds to the visual interest of the frame. The smooth opaque curves of gold seem to float above this choppy surface, all the more refined by contrast. Precision matters not one bit when painting the gold detailing, but an easy, fluent line is all-important. It may help to practice first on a piece of paper, just to loosen up your brushstrokes.

The birds decorating this frame are stylized and quite simple, but again, practice will help you achieve sinuous perfection of beak and feather. Finally, the putty surrounding the mirror needs careful molding to look good − if you doubt your ability to produce even undulations, you could decorate it with a textured stamped pattern, using the prongs of a fork.

Aegean Blue
This well-behaved line of elegant golden birds has Greek origins, while the blue of the frame conjures up images of sun-warmed sea and little fishing boats. Not many mirror frames can do this.

A Mirror with a Message
It is not easy to decipher, but this beautiful rhythmic script on its marbled background was achieved after a great deal of practice for fluency, using a fine sable brush. The putty rim is decorated with beads.

Making and Decorating the Frame

*Elegant golden birds, looking very like the Egyptian sun god,
Ra, parade in a never-ending circle beneath an ultramarine sky.*

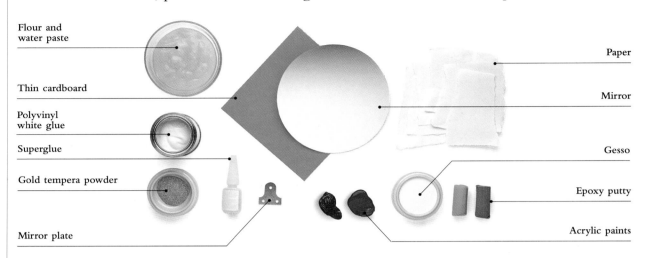

Flour and water paste

Thin cardboard

Polyvinyl white glue

Superglue

Gold tempera powder

Mirror plate

Paper

Mirror

Gesso

Epoxy putty

Acrylic paints

1 *Cut out a large circle of paper, wet it with water to prevent sticking, and lay it on a work surface. Cover it with 20 layers of paper, pasted on with flour and water paste. Leave to dry. The edges of the circle will curl up slightly when drying. When dry, cover both sides of the paper circle with a coat of gesso to provide a smooth surface for decorating with paints.*

2 *When the gesso is dry, draw around the mirror in the center of the circle with a pencil. Paint the outer edge of the paper circle with phthalo-green acrylic paint.*

3 *Using a pair of compasses, draw a circle on the cardboard that is larger than the size of the mirror, but smaller than the size of the paper circle. Divide it up into equal sections using the compasses and a ruler. Cut out a circle in the middle – the size of the mirror – and draw a simple repeating bird outline in each of the outer sections. Cut out the bird template.*

4 *Place the template on the paper circle, matching up the central circles. Using an artist's brush dipped in gold tempera powder mixed with water, paint the outline of the birds, using the template as a guide.*

5 *Paint the inner rim surrounding the mirror area, and the outer rim of the paper circle, with dilute ultramarine acrylic paint. Paint the outer rim with wavy lines, following the shapes of the birds.*

6 *Add the finer detailing on the bird shapes. Using an artist's brush and gold tempera powder mixed with water, paint on eyes, wings, and feathers.*

7 *When the paint has dried, glue the mirror to the center of the paper frame using polyvinyl glue. Roll out a long "snake" of epoxy putty and stick this around the edge of the mirror. Press into place with your thumbs to create a decorative impression (see inset).*

8 *Paint the putty rim with gold tempera powder mixed with water. Paint the back of the frame with a coat of ultramarine acrylic paint to seal it. Let the frame dry for a couple of hours, then glue a mirror plate to the back of the frame using a strong glue.*

Tiny Hooked Frame

MATERIALS

Thin cardboard
Burlap
Assorted fabric strips,
¾in (2cm) wide
Latex adhesive
Clear adhesive
Black felt
Black sewing thread
Drink can ring-tab
Picture glass or mirror

EQUIPMENT

Black marker
Embroidery frame
Hook
Scissors
Needle
Pins

O NCE UPON A TIME, country fireside and kitchen rugs were made from the worn-out woolens and petticoats accumulated throughout the year. Cut into strips by one of the younger members of the family, they would be prodded or hooked through a backing of burlap bags, a process that occupied a winter and took place annually. These rag rugs would greet the world at the front door, or bring warmth and cheer to the hearth. They were not made to last forever, and with each passing year would be demoted from parlor to kitchen, finally ending up in the animal bed.

These days, no one has the time or inclination to recycle on this scale, and for most people there is, thankfully, no longer an urgent necessity to make do and mend. However, hooked rags have a texture and personality unlike anything else and are surprisingly easy to make. This witty little frame is made from pieces of man-made fabric acquired at thrift stores – it could be the perfect frame for the family tree. Who knows, you may get hooked yourself, and become a rug addict in time.

Crimplene and Coronets

Hooking rugs is habit-forming – it is one of those soothing, mindless activities that puts problems in a less panicky perspective. Start with an almost instant witty trifle, like this crowned frame, and you will soon find yourself at work on a baronial hearth rug for the east wing.

Rag Time

An irreverent pastiche of pomp and circumstance, these rags are nothing if not regal – a royal purple, lime green, and red crown and a fleur-de-lis in candy-colored fabrics. Just the thing to frame your graduation diploma.

Making and Decorating the Frame

This little frame is a recycler's dream – even the hanging hook is made from a soft drink ring-tab.

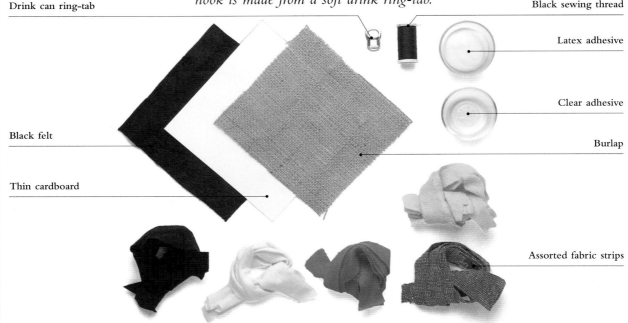

Drink can ring-tab

Black sewing thread

Latex adhesive

Clear adhesive

Black felt

Burlap

Thin cardboard

Assorted fabric strips

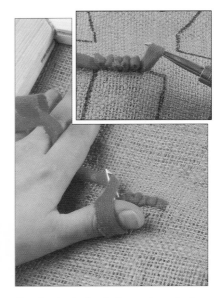

1 *Make a cardboard template of the shape of frame you require. Using a marker, draw around the template onto the burlap, leaving a border of at least 3in (7.5cm) around the design. Attach the burlap to the embroidery frame.*

2 *Hold a fabric strip underneath the burlap, and push the hook through the burlap from the top. Guide the fabric strip over the hook to create a loop. Pull the hook back up through the burlap, bringing the end of the fabric strip to the top.*

3 *Push the hook down through the burlap again, just next to the first loop, guide the fabric onto the hook, and pull through the fabric to the top side to form a loop on the surface (see inset). Pull the strip back until the loop is the required height.*

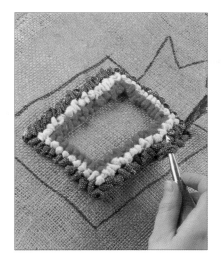

4 *Continue forming rows of loops to fill the area of the frame. When you reach the end of a fabric strip, bring the end through to the top side and trim to the height of the loops. Change to another color of fabric when desired.*

5 *Remove the burlap from the frame and lay it facedown on a flat surface. Cut the excess burlap away to leave a border around the frame of 2in (5cm). Using a piece of cardboard, smear a thin layer of latex adhesive over the back of the frame.*

6 *Using scissors, make diagonal cuts in the burlap into the corners of the frame, right up to the hooked area, and fold in the edges, squeezing the corners together. Trim off the excess fabric.*

7 *Make diagonal cuts in the burlap in the central picture area, from corner to corner. Fold each resulting triangular flap back onto the glued area. Let dry for 30 minutes.*

8 *Apply a thin layer of clear adhesive onto the back of the frame and place the frame glued-side down on a piece of black felt. Trim the edges of the felt, then carefully cut out the central picture area. Using black sewing thread, slip stitch the felt to the burlap around all the edges to fasten. Let dry for two hours.*

9 *Cut out a piece of black felt to make a pocket in which to slip the picture glass or mirror. Pin onto the reverse of the frame, centering it over the picture area. Using black sewing thread, blanket stitch the pocket in place, then sew a drink can ring-tab securely onto the back of the frame for the hanging hook (see inset).*

Brilliant Tissue Frame

MATERIALS

Powder paint
Matte acrylic
copolymer latex paint
Acid-free plain and
decorated tissue paper
Metallic powder
Particleboard, ½in
(12mm) thick
Acrylic paints
Matte acrylic
gel medium
Polyvinyl white glue
Dark blue latex paint
Wooden dowelling
Mirror
Cardboard
Nails
2 hanging hooks
Decorative cord

EQUIPMENT

Housepainter's brush
Artist's brush
Pencil
Jigsaw
Ruler
Hammer

A T FIRST SIGHT, it is impossible to tell what this frame is made of: layer upon layer of rich color and gold make it as sumptuous as an Indian palace, and as richly textured as scagliola. The opulent irregular surface is held within carefully delineated borders and outlines, a contrast between materials and method that works to their mutual flattery. The components of the frame have a sense of discipline, despite being less than symmetrical, while the shape is unique, with all the arches and complexities of an Islamic gateway. Altogether, this mirror frame achieves the utterly exotic using deceptively simple means.

The secret of this frame's success is the subtle layering of related colors – there is nothing jarring or glaring in this palette. The effect of using autumnal browns and russets together would be equally successful. For a different look, the frame could be used to show off a wood-blocked motif, printed in cinnabar red on textured cream paper. This is a glorious frame – it would look good against a plain white wall, but is also strong enough to hold its own with paisley and rich ethnic textiles, or lively distemper-type paint.

High-Impact Color

As opulently exotic as the riches of the Casbah, this frame is a tribute to the sizzling potential of paint and tissue paper. A mixture of spontaneity and control governs the buildup of color, and assembling the collage is a miracle of casual deftness.

Spectrum Exploration
Small changes in shape emphasize the discipline that holds together the kaleidoscope of color adorning each of these frames. Without discreet but insistent control, these visual symphonies could easily become chaotic cacophony.

70

Making and Decorating the Frame

Customized tissue paper in rich peacock colors makes this frame truly sumptuous.

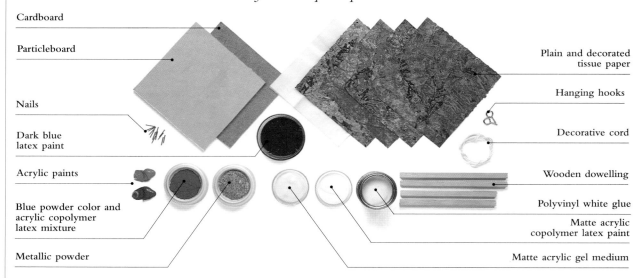

Cardboard

Particleboard

Nails

Dark blue latex paint

Acrylic paints

Blue powder color and acrylic copolymer latex mixture

Metallic powder

Plain and decorated tissue paper

Hanging hooks

Decorative cord

Wooden dowelling

Polyvinyl white glue

Matte acrylic copolymer latex paint

Matte acrylic gel medium

1 *Mix 10 parts powder color with 1 part matte acrylic copolymer latex and dilute with water to the consistency of cream. Paint this onto plain tissue paper. When dry, apply paler colors and then metallic powder mixed with matte acrylic copolymer latex, rolling the brush over the paper to produce random patterns (see inset). Allow to dry.*

2 *Draw out the shape of the frame on particleboard. It can be a simple square or circle, or, as here, an arch with extra pieces jutting out for added interest. Cut out the frame with a jigsaw.*

3 *Paint areas of blue, purple, and green acrylic paint to cover the frame base and allow to dry.*

4 *Draw a rectangle around the inner frame to provide a guideline when gluing on tissue paper. Paste overlapping strips of decorated tissue paper onto the frame using matte acrylic gel medium. Add as many layers as desired for color and texture.*

5 *Paste more strips of decorated tissue paper in similar shades around the central part of the frame, following the pencil guideline.*

6 *Cut out a second piece of particleboard, larger than the opening in the frame, to make the inner frame. Cut out a central area for the mirror. Cover this inner frame with decorated tissue paper, pasting it down with matte acrylic gel medium. Fold the tissue back around the inner edge to reveal the mirror area. Glue this inner frame to the outer frame using polyvinyl glue. Leave to dry overnight with a weight on top.*

7 *Paste on more tissue as desired. Here thin side strips and an arch highlight the shape of the frame. Let dry before painting the back of the frame with dark blue latex paint. When dry, glue four pieces of wooden dowelling around the mirror opening on the back of the frame. Place the mirror in this dowelling holder, lay backing cardboard on top (see inset), and tack in place with nails (see p.9). Add hanging hooks and cord as required (see p.9).*

Pure Fabrication

MATERIALS

Thick cardboard
Corrugated cardboard
Mirror tile
Masking tape
Cotton fabric
Contrasting
cotton fabric
Polyvinyl white glue
Embroidery thread
Curtain ring
Braid trim

EQUIPMENT

Felt-tip pen
Craft knife
Ruler
Scissors
Needle
Pins

THESE FABRIC–COVERED FRAMES would contribute style and opulence to any room. They are perfectly straightforward to make and employ only the most basic materials – remnants of cloth, pieces of braid trim, and cardboard backing.

There are no limitations of size, shape, or color with this simple technique. Minaret shapes and strong spice colors look magnificent massed among Indian block-printed textiles; classic squares or rectangles suit plainer interiors. A circular chintz frame hung from a bow would look at home in a woman's bedroom, while a triangular frame trimmed with plaid fabric and finished with brass studs would reflect a manly visage without causing embarrassment. Striped ticking would look fresh and clean; bright spots could be a cure for vanity. For a more sumptuous look, experiment with upholstery fabrics – velvet and brocade would lend Renaissance richness to the most humble hall.

Paisley Casbah
This pretty silhouette is reminiscent of the dome of an Indian palace. It is covered with vibrant red paisley cloth and is finished with decorative braid and a complementary slice of green fabric.

Perfect Adaptability
Shaded fabrics make a terrific ensemble. If a multitude of mirrors strikes you as being too much of a good thing, you can echo or contrast the dominant color of postcards, paintings, or photographs to frame them in splendor.

Making and Decorating the Frame

*The fabric is attached to the frame using polyvinyl glue.
When applying this, take care not to spill it on the surface
of the mirror because it may destroy the finish. If you do
spill any glue, wipe it off immediately with a damp cloth.*

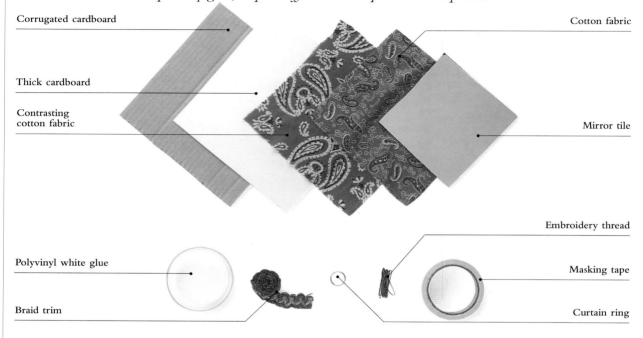

Corrugated cardboard

Thick cardboard

Contrasting
cotton fabric

Cotton fabric

Mirror tile

Embroidery thread

Polyvinyl white glue

Masking tape

Braid trim

Curtain ring

1 *Make a cardboard template
of an arch. Draw around this
template on corrugated cardboard
and thick cardboard and cut out five
shapes: three from corrugated, and two
from thick cardboard. Cut a window
out of the middle of one of the thick
cardboard arches, 12mm (1/2 in)
smaller all around than the mirror tile.*

2 *Draw around the mirror tile
in the middle of one of the
corrugated cardboard arches. Using
a craft knife, cut out and discard the
central piece of cardboard and replace
with the mirror tile. Secure the tile
with masking tape around all the
edges, both on the front and the back
of the cardboard.*

3 *Place the two thick cardboard
arches on the two contrasting
fabrics. Cut around the edges, leaving
a 1¼in (3cm) border all around. Set
aside one piece of fabric. Cut out a
window from the other piece, leaving a
¾in (2cm) border. Snip the fabric into
the corners and glue the edges onto the
cardboard using polyvinyl glue.*

4 *Cut out four strips of contrasting fabric, 1½in (4cm) wide and the length of the mirror tile. Fold each strip in half lengthwise and press to create a neat edge. Using polyvinyl glue, glue each strip to the back of the arch along each edge of the window, overlapping the window slightly so that you can see a narrow strip of the fabric on the right side of the frame.*

5 *Using embroidery thread, oversew or use blanket stitching to attach a curtain ring to the upper center of the second piece of fabric. Because the ring will be the means of hanging the frame, make sure that the stitching is secure. Remember to stitch around only half of the ring — the other half will be used as the hook.*

6 *Place the fabric ring-side down. Using polyvinyl glue, glue one corrugated cardboard arch to the remaining thick cardboard arch. Place these glued pieces on the fabric with the thick cardboard underneath and wrap the fabric over the edges. Snip around the curves of the arch with scissors and glue the fabric in place with polyvinyl glue.*

7 *Glue the front of the frame to the two remaining corrugated cardboard arches (this is to prevent the mirror from coming into contact with the polyvinyl glue, because the glue will destroy the silver finish on the mirror). Then sandwich the front and back pieces of the frame together with polyvinyl glue. Place the frame under a heavy weight for several hours to dry thoroughly.*

8 *Glue decorative braid trim around the edges of the frame, cutting it to fit at the joint. Pin the braid to the frame to hold it in place while it is drying. Remove the pins when the glue has dried. Finally, give the mirror a quick cleaning to remove any marks.*

Gothic Mirror

MATERIALS

Tracing paper
Thick corrugated cardboard
Polyvinyl white glue
Newsprint
Wallpaper paste
Black acrylic paint
Length of wood two-thirds the width of the frame
Mirror
Mirror adhesive
String
Modeling clay
White latex paint
Dark gray undercoat paint
Dark blue gloss paint
Gold acrylic paint
2 D-ring hangers and screws

EQUIPMENT

Pencil
Craft knife
Metal ruler
Artist's brush
Housepainter's brush
Sponge
Small dish
Screwdriver

THIS SPLENDID MIRROR is perfect for Count Dracula to check that no shred of spinach mars his postprandial canines before going out for the evening. This is a mirror frame with gravitas, whose intricate construction completely supersedes its humble constituents. Despite its considerable size, this frame is made from nothing more grandiose than corrugated cardboard, and is surprisingly lightweight and portable.

To reinforce the frame's air of grave antiquity, you could use a mottled and ancient-looking glass and distress the paintwork a little. It would look superb in a baronial setting, ideally with crenellated turrets – perhaps in a gothic arched hallway where it could reflect the flickering light from beeswax candles in an iron candlestick, or a couple of wolfhounds stretched-out before a tree trunk that is blazing in the fireplace. Alternatively, its dignified masculinity and witty relish for pastiche would be quite at home reflecting white walls and designer furniture in a warehouse or loft apartment.

Brooding Magnificence
This is a mirror frame to live up to, an aspirational beginning until you can afford the mortgage on the castle. Ideally it should be flanked by a halberd, some chain mail, and your jousting equipment.

Crenellations in Cardboard
A russet version of the heraldic mirror, complete with turrets, star, crest, and crenellations. This frame is awkward to make, but the effort is handsomely rewarded.

Making and Decorating the Frame
A handsome and bold mirror — plain miraculous when you realize that it is made of nothing more heroic than corrugated cardboard.

Mirror adhesive

Length of wood

Corrugated cardboard

Newsprint

Thick cardboard

D-ring hangers and screws

White latex paint

Wallpaper paste

Polyvinyl white glue

Black acrylic paint

Gold acrylic paint

Modeling clay

String

Dark blue gloss paint

Dark gray undercoat paint

1 *Photocopy the templates for the frame (see pp. 92–3) to the required size, and trace templates A to I onto corrugated cardboard. Trace templates K and L onto thick cardboard. Using a craft knife and metal ruler for the straight edges, cut out all the components. You should have a total of 14 pieces cut from corrugated cardboard; the number of pieces cut from thick cardboard — the bricks — will depend on the size of frame you make.*

2 *Using polyvinyl glue, glue the two side pieces (E) onto the front piece (D). Paste strips of torn newsprint over the inside edge using wallpaper paste. Paint the underside of the inside edge with black acrylic paint to prevent the cardboard from being reflected in the mirror.*

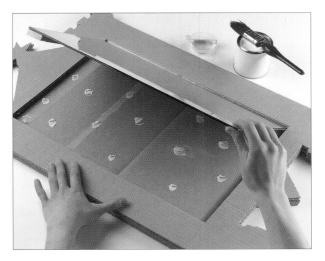

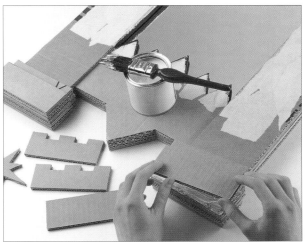

3 Glue the wood onto the top edge of the mirror back using mirror adhesive. Following the diagram on p.93, assemble the frame. First glue the back pieces (A and B) and center piece (C) together with polyvinyl glue. Insert the mirror into the center piece and attach with mirror adhesive. Mark the position of the wood on the back of the frame (this is where D-ring hangers will be attached).

4 Using polyvinyl glue, paste the front piece (D) over the mirror. Attach two steps (I and H) to the base of each side piece. Then glue the battlements (F) to the top of each side piece and the star (G) to the center top of the frame. Using wallpaper paste, paste three or four layers of torn overlapping pieces of newsprint over the entire mirror frame and allow to dry.

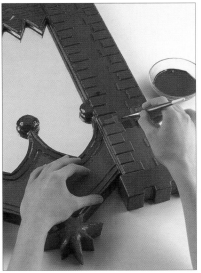

5 Add decorative details to the frame. Glue string around the edges of the center panel. Mold a raised star, raised bosses, and a fleur-de-lis (J) from modeling clay and glue in position in the center panel. Glue bricks (K and L) down the edges of the two sides, alternating longer and shorter bricks.

6 Paint the whole frame with several layers of white latex paint to seal. When dry, apply a coat of dark gray undercoat and finally a coat of dark blue gloss paint. Allow to dry.

7 Dip a sponge in gold acrylic paint, dab off the excess in a small dish, then dab the sponge over the raised areas of the frame, including the bricks, star, bosses, fleur-de-lis, and steps. When dry, screw two D-ring hangers into the back of frame at the position of the wood marked earlier (see inset).

Gilded Velvet Frame

MATERIALS

14in (35cm) square
of paper

14in (35cm) square
of velvet

2 x 12in (30cm)
squares of fabric

Multidyed rayon
thread

Torn strips of blue
and orange silk,
½in (12mm) wide

Polyvinyl white glue

Mirror tile

2 x 10in (25cm)
squares of corrugated
cardboard

Gold enamel paint

Masking tape

EQUIPMENT

Felt-tip pen

Ruler

Pins

Tailor's chalk

Sewing machine

Small sharp scissors

2 housepainter's
brushes

Craft knife

FOR TOTAL OPULENCE, this is a difficult frame to beat. The raw materials alone look like Aladdin's cave, with a wealth of color and texture that just makes you want to touch. A hoarder's heaven, this frame is a handsome vindication of a lifetime of collecting scraps and remnants, and could be the glorious final resting place for the ribbons from Christmas packages that were too wonderful to throw away. But you must be bold; the dramatic impact of this frame owes much to the casual imprecision with which it was put together. If you try too hard and measure too exactly, the frame will end up prim and fussy.

Using fabric has one great advantage – you can try out different combinations of color, texture, and pattern before you begin. Here the formula is a sumptuous mixture of silks and velvet, and there is a definite element of Spanish baroque. You could go seriously wild and use golden tassels, mirror glass, sequins, braid trim, and beads. Or you might find that plainer, homespun materials suit your home. Let your feeling for the fabrics guide you.

Baroque Splendor
There are times when everybody needs a touch of glamour. The trick is to be unafraid of it. If glamour is your goal, go all out for it with sensuous flocked walls, swaths of sumptuous velvet and golden flowers. Don't apologize, enjoy!

Sumptuous Remnants
There are as many permutations on a theme of satin and silk, velvet and gold, as your remnants, research, and energy allow. Look to Gothic architecture and Elizabethan costume for inspiration.

Making and Decorating the Frame

Create a kaleidoscope of color and texture by using scraps from the motley collection of fabric in your workbasket to make a frame. This provides a great way to use up fabric that is too pretty to throw away.

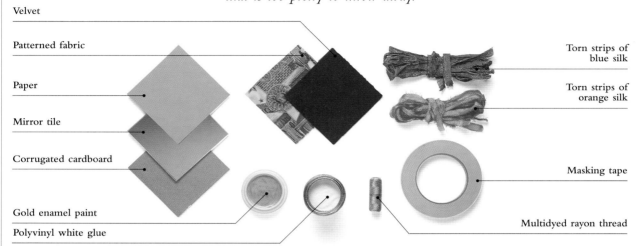

Velvet

Patterned fabric

Paper

Mirror tile

Corrugated cardboard

Gold enamel paint

Polyvinyl white glue

Torn strips of blue silk

Torn strips of orange silk

Masking tape

Multidyed rayon thread

1 *Draw the design of the frame on paper using a felt-tip pen. Here the design is a simple symmetrical pattern of straight lines and curved edges. Pin the wrong side of the velvet square to the right side of one of the patterned fabric squares. Transfer the design from the paper onto the velvet using tailor's chalk (see inset).*

2 *Using a sewing machine threaded with multidyed rayon thread, sew two rows of straight stitches around the chalked lines. Stitch around the edge of the square with zigzag stitches.*

3 *Using small scissors, cut out alternating sections of velvet around the outer edge of the square to reveal the patterned fabric beneath. Cut close to the lines of stitching, without cutting the actual threads of the stitches.*

4 *Stitch strips of torn blue silk around the cut edges to outline the velvet. When one strip comes to an end, simply but the next strip to this edge and continue stitching.*

5 *Stitch strips of torn orange silk up and down the inner semicircles of the velvet, to make triangular-shaped blocks. Use either the straight stitch foot or the embroidery foot on the sewing machine. Cut out the center of the fabric squares.*

6 *Using a housepainter's brush, paint polyvinyl glue over the surface of the fabric. Let dry until the glue becomes transparent. Lightly brush gold enamel paint across the surface, so that it just catches the raised areas of the fabric (see inset).*

7 *Using a craft knife, cut out the center of one square of cardboard the size of the mirror tile. Insert the mirror tile in the opening and secure with masking tape. Brush polyvinyl glue on the cardboard around the mirror, then place it glue-side down onto the reverse of the painted fabric square, making sure that the mirror is aligned with the opening in the fabric. Trim the patterned fabric back to the edge of the cardboard and brush glue over the velvet. Fold the velvet edges over the cardboard, and press them down.*

8 *Glue a square of patterned fabric to the remaining cardboard square, folding the ends over. With fabric facing outward, glue the two squares of the frame together using polyvinyl glue. If desired, sew a curtain ring onto the back of the frame as a hanging hook (see p.77).*

Ideas to Inspire

Paper and fabric frames can be extremely inventive and a great excuse to have fun. This section encourages you to be adventurous with hand hooking, machine embroidery, papier-mâché, decoupage, and batik, all of which can form the basis of or add decoration to a frame.

▶ **Padded Silk Frame**
Inspired by Islamic and Indian jewelry, this decorative mirror frame is made from silk, embellished with appliquéd shapes and decorative stitching, then stuffed with batting to complete.

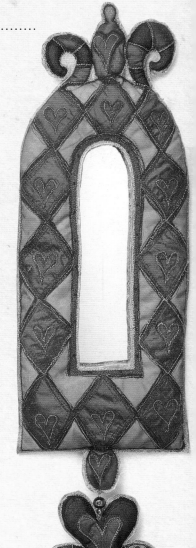

▲ **Papier–Mâché Aviary**
Featuring stylized bird motifs, this colorful papier mâché-frame is made by smoothing paper pulp over a cardboard base, then decorating with crayons for a broken texture.

◀ **Hooked Rag Bag**
A delightfully fresh and contemporary approach to the centuries-old tradition of hand hooking, this decorative mirror frame, made from red, yellow, and blue fabric scraps, is good irreverent fun and very quick to make.

▶ Gilded for Glamour
Not a frame for the faint-hearted, this splendid creation would bring instant glamour to your home. Made from hardboard and paper pulp, it is decorated with oil-based paint and gold metal leaf.

▲ Pretty Paperwork
Painstakingly constructed from pieces of wood glued and pegged together, this highly decorative box cupboard is covered with several layers of ripped paper decorated with oil paints and inks. Copper and brass provide extra embellishment.

◀ Electric Color
This multicolored frame, with its integral central artwork, is made from laminated board covered with watercolor paper that has been dyed with acid-reactive dyes and decorated with penwork. Quilled paper scrolls add extra interest.

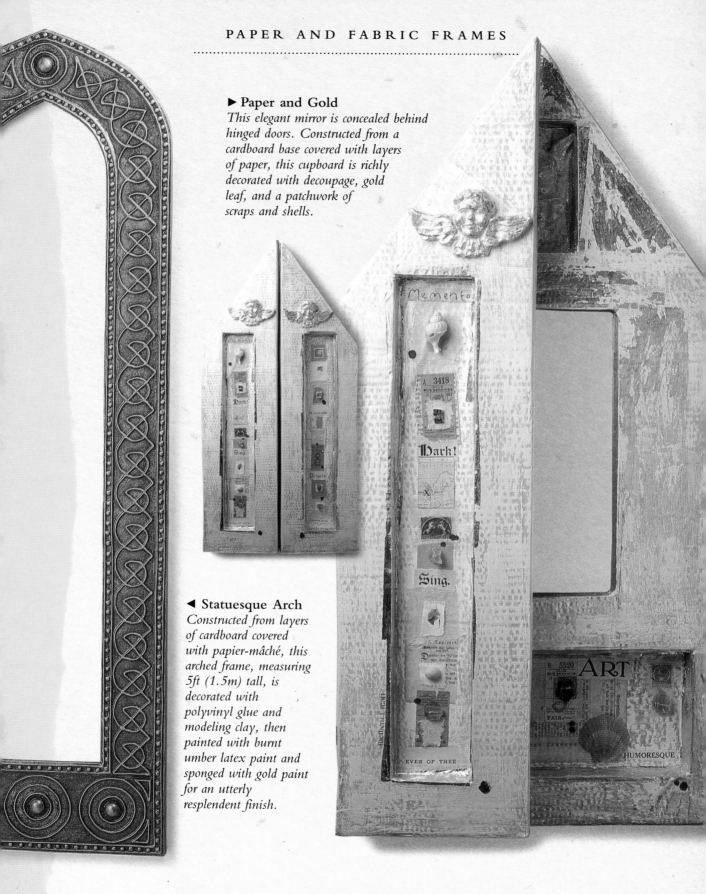

▶ Paper and Gold
This elegant mirror is concealed behind hinged doors. Constructed from a cardboard base covered with layers of paper, this cupboard is richly decorated with decoupage, gold leaf, and a patchwork of scraps and shells.

◀ Statuesque Arch
Constructed from layers of cardboard covered with papier-mâché, this arched frame, measuring 5ft (1.5m) tall, is decorated with polyvinyl glue and modeling clay, then painted with burnt umber latex paint and sponged with gold paint for an utterly resplendent finish.

▼ Edged with Silver

This stylish frame is easily made by gluing decorated handmade papers onto a plain wooden frame. The inner edge of the frame is then gilded with silver leaf and the whole frame is sealed with varnish.

▶ Palladian Classic

Inspired by classical architecture, this impressive arched frame is constructed from corrugated cardboard covered with layers of newsprint, then sponged all over in somber shades of gray latex paint.

▼ Batik Frame

Using hand-painted fabric for decoration, this wooden frame is first sprayed with car paint, then the batik-dyed fabric is glued in position and the entire frame sealed with clear waterproof varnish.

▲ Wreathed in Ivy

This inventive papier-mâché frame is decorated with ivy leaves, each made from several layers of paper glued together and attached to the frame with wire to stand out in relief.

Templates

Shown here are the templates for four of the projects featured earlier in the book. Enlarge the templates to the required size on a photocopier, keeping all the templates from one project in proportion to each other.

Rustic Chicken Frame
(p. 40)

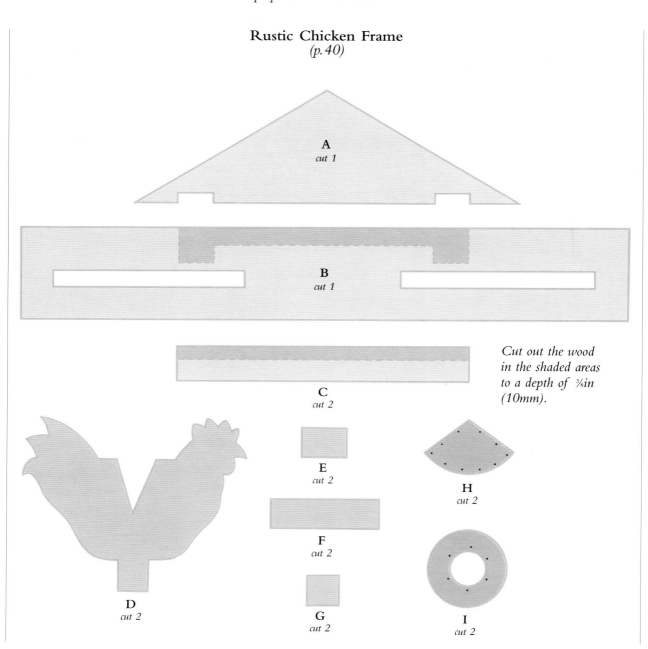

A
cut 1

B
cut 1

C
cut 2

Cut out the wood in the shaded areas to a depth of ⅜in (10mm).

E
cut 2

H
cut 2

F
cut 2

D
cut 2

G
cut 2

I
cut 2

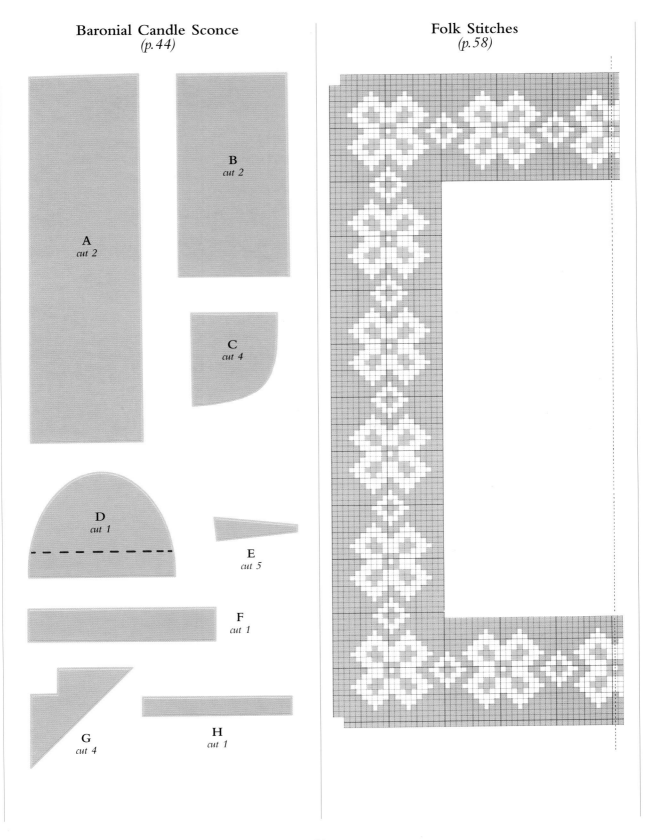

Baronial Candle Sconce
(p.44)

A
cut 2

B
cut 2

C
cut 4

D
cut 1

E
cut 5

F
cut 1

G
cut 4

H
cut 1

Folk Stitches
(p.58)

Gothic Mirror
(p. 78)

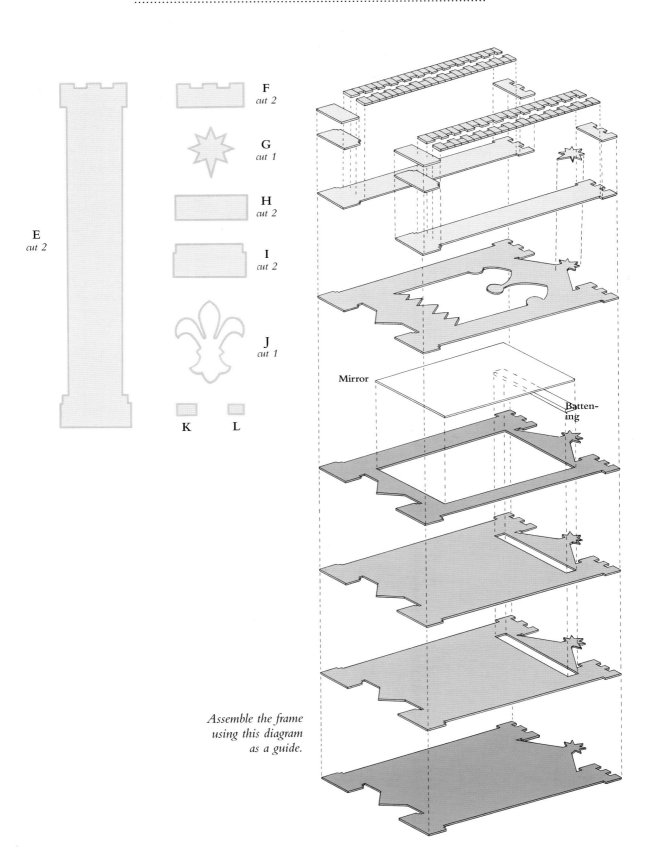

E
cut 2

F
cut 2

G
cut 1

H
cut 2

I
cut 2

J
cut 1

K   L

Mirror

Batten-
ing

*Assemble the frame
using this diagram
as a guide.*

Contributors

The Author,
pp. 12-15; pp. 20-23.

Madeleine Adams,
p. 86 center.

Sonia Akow,
pp. 24-27; p. 51 bottom right.

Clare Bawcutt,
p. 50 bottom.

Alison Britton,
p. 89 bottom right.

Patrick Burton,
pp. 70-73.

Ann Carter,
p. 89 bottom center.

Martin Cheek,
pp. 36-39.

Jason Cleverly,
p. 48 top.

Patricia Crowther,
p. 49 center.

Hazel Dolby,
p. 88 bottom right.

Amanda Foot,
pp. 40-43.

Ann Frith,
pp. 54-57; p. 87 bottom right.

Victor Stuart Graham,
p. 50 top left.

Gigi Griffiths,
pp. 74-77.

Tony Isseyegh,
p. 51 center.

Paul Johnson,
p. 86 bottom right.

Andrea Maflin,
p. 89 top left.

Lorna Moffat,
pp. 82-85.

Helen Musselwhite,
pp. 28-31; p. 51 top right.

Cleo Mussi,
p. 49 right.

Mary Norden,
pp. 58-61.

Sarah Parish,
pp. 16-19.

Maxine Pharoah,
pp. 50-51 top center.

Mandy Pritty,
pp. 48-49 bottom.

Trisha Rafferty,
p. 48 center.

Lizzie Reakes,
pp. 66-69; p. 86 bottom left.

Carolyn Sansbury,
pp. 62-65.

Jackie Shelton,
p. 88 top right.

Claire Sowden,
p. 86 top right.

Eleanor Staley,
pp. 78-81; p. 88 left; p. 89 top right.

Alison Start,
pp. 44-47.

James Taylor,
pp. 32-35.

Juliet Walker,
p. 87 top left.

Steve Wright,
p. 49 top.

Index

A

acetate 20, 28–31
ageing 8, 11, 12, 15,
    51, 78
arched frames 49, 76,
    88
assembly 9

B

baronial candle sconce
    44–47, 91
batik 89
beads 31
beeswax 26, 46
beveled edges 8, 9
blackening cream 47
box frames 48, 49
brilliant tissue frame
    70–73

C

candle wax 14
candlesticks 40–43,
    44–47
cardboard 6, 28–31, 76,
    78, 80, 84, 86–89
clamps 9
collage 7, 11, 48
combing technique 9
cord 8, 9
craquelure 11, 15

D

decoupage 6–7, 11,
    12–15, 88
distressed effects 27, 78
dragging 8, 11
driftwood 6, 7, 40, 48,
    49, 50
    and seashells 16–19
dyes 24, 87, 89

E

equipment 8, 44

F

fabric frames 53, 58–61,
    66–69, 74–77, 82–85
    suggestions 86, 89
finishes 8–9, 11
fishes and squiggles 54–57
flour and water paste 62
foil 6, 11, 28–31, 49
folk stitches 58–61, 91

G

gilded velvet frame 82–85
glass jewels 6, 11, 28, 36
glazed wood 24–27
glittering trail 36–39
glue 8, 31, 40, 76
    flour and water paste
      62
    latex 68
gold
    foil 49
    leaf 88
    metal leaf 87
    paint 32, 48, 51, 81, 85
    powder 23
    tempera powder 65
golden birds mirror 62–65
gothic mirror 78–81,
    92–93
grout 36–39

H

hanging hooks 8, 68, 77
hooked rags 7, 66–69, 86

I

ideas to inspire
    paper and fabric 86–89
    wood and metal 48–51
ink 24

J

jeweled silver frame
    28–31

L

lacquer finish 11
lettering 7, 48, 58

M

mat board 8, 9
mat cutters 8
materials 6–7, 8
measuring 8
metal frames 11, 40,
    44–47, 50–51
    suggestions 50–51
    tools 44
metal leaf 87
metallic powder 72
mirrors 6
    arched 49, 76
    baronial candle sconce
      44–47
    doors 44, 88
    fabric-covered frames
      74–77
    gilded velvet frame
      82–85
    golden birds 62–65
    gothic 78–81, 92–93
    heart-shaped 49
    mosaic 36–39
    rustic chicken 40–43
    silver-leafed 24
mitering 7, 8–9
molding 8, 32–35
mosaic 7, 11, 36–39,
    49, 50

N

needlepoint 50, 58–61

P

packing tape 9
padded silk frame 86
paint
    acrylic 64, 72, 80
    car 89
    gesso 48, 64
    gloss 80
    latex 14, 23, 72, 80
    oil 15, 43
    oil-based 32, 56
    powder 70
    techniques 8–9
    water-based 24
    watercolor 51
paper frames 53–57,
    62–65, 70–73, 78–82
    suggestions 86–89
paper pulp 56
papier-mâché 7, 53
    bird motifs 86
    fishes and squiggles
      54–57
    golden birds 62–65
    ivy leaves 89
    statuesque arch 88
particleboard 36, 51,
    70–73
patchwork 20, 53, 58
pebbles 16
plywood 40, 54
polish 24, 46
pure fabrication 74–77
putty 62

R

ragging 9
rope 18
rustic chicken frame
    40–43, 90

S

sanding 8, 14, 27
sconces 40, 44–47, 91
shells 16–19, 49, 88

silver
  leaf 89
  metal leaf 57
smalti 36-39, 50
stain 24, 32
stars and hearts 20-23
stencils 8, 9, 11, 20-23,
    35, 51
stippling 11, 35, 43

T
tapestry 20, 58-61
techniques 8-9
templates 90-93
tiny hooked frame 66-69
tissue paper 7, 70-73
tools 8, 44
tortoiseshell 9
touches of gold 32-35

V
varnish
  craquelure 11, 15
  gloss 56
  water-based 20
verdigris effect 8, 11

W
wood filler 32, 34
wood frames 11-43
  finishes 11
  suggestions 48-51
woodgraining 24

Acknowledgments

This book owes just about everything to the talent and generosity of the many frame-makers whose work it shows. Craftspeople are an endangered species and eke out a precarious living. I hope this book will tempt you to share the satisfaction and fun that they enjoy.

The people who turned the ravishing raw material into a book were Clive Streeter who took the pictures and personifies patience, endurance and ingenuity; Marnie Searchwell who made sure they looked good and contributed a sure hand and fastidious quality control; Ali Edney, the ariel of stylists, who sped over unimaginable distances in her quest for props; and Heather Dewhurst who did the most difficult thing of all – composed the haiku of step-by-step instructions, along with some mettlesome editing.

Stuart Stevenson of the excellent eponymous shop let us make free with his paints and papers. Roger Bristow effected one or two daring rescues, and Sarah Hoggett kept the whole unruly caravan behaving as it ought. Finally, Kate Haxell and Claire Worthington contributed more than they thought.